AND A GOOD JOB TOO

AND A
GOOD JOB TOO

DAVID MACKINTOSH

ORION

First published in Great Britain in 1993 by Orion
An imprint of Orion Books Ltd
Orion House, 5 Upper St Martin's Lane, London WC2H 9EA

A CIP catalogue record for this book is available
from the British Library
ISBN 1 85797 124 8 (csd)
ISBN 1 85797 248 1 (tpb)

Typeset by Datix International Limited, Bungay, Suffolk
Printed in Great Britain by Clays Ltd, St Ives plc

This book is for
Charles, Elissa, Robert and Sheela,
tho' I hope that none of them ever has to read it

Contents

14 Eyeball to Eyeball   137

Interviews * the interviewer wants you to do well * preparation
* your own PR material * dress * smoking * punctuality * the
aim * instant reaction * discussing the job * questions * tell me
about yourself * why are you looking for a job? * why you? *
variations on a theme * unanswerable questions * invasion of
privacy? * logistics * rewards * location * availability *
subsequent interviews and short-lists * AOB * a quarterback
option play * what next? * expenses

15 Trial by Jury   157

Extending the decision-making * are one-to-one interviews
valid? * large organisations * panel interviews * assessment
centres * get hold of the marker pen

16 Handling Those Offers . . . and Those Rejections   162

Rejections are inevitable * advertised jobs – rejection during
screening * flannel * refusals to meet * rejection after first
interview * rejection after short-list * a success story * success
– an offer at last * the perfect job * a poor job * the delaying
game * the ultimate question

17 As the Sun Sinks Slowly in the West   170

Still work to do * relax * stand down your network * review
your life * *valete*

Acknowledgements

My thanks to:

First of all my outplacement patients, who have bullied and cajoled me into writing this book. Their contributions to the development of ideas about the fascinating art of job-hunting have been invaluable. I hope that Brian Winch will not take offence if I describe him as the Head Bully.

Jacintha Alexander, writers' agent, who had the gullibility or astuteness – the choice is yours – to respond to my original proposal for this book, which would not have reached the start line without her enthusiasm and expertise.

Rosie Cheetham, who has guided me through the potentially glamorous but daunting world of book publishing, confirming the former perception whilst refuting the latter.

Katie Pope of Orion Books, whose contribution at times of stress – and inevitably producing a book causes moments of stress for a virgin author – was superlative. Her composure and efficiency were invaluable.

Jeff Abbott, ex-colleague and long-term friend, who won the 'name my book' competition. The first prize was a mention (this is it) and a case of something palatable – which has been duly delivered.

All those who have given me permission to quote from their published or unpublished writings, or who have otherwise provided input. They are, in alphabetical order (but not putting ladies first, lest I appear not to be Politically Correct): Brian Armitage, Charles Bremner, Brenda Bruce, Max Hastings, Lee Iacocca (through the good offices of Bantam), Virginia Ironside, Brian Steptoe and Margaret Wallis.

BBC Education in general, and Liz Barclay in particular, for permitting me to lift the whole list of useful addresses and phone numbers which was included in the excellent pamphlet 'Work it Out', published in January 1993.

Pat Berry, without whom neither Mackintosh Enterprises nor this book would exist. She ran my office in the 3i days at Windsor and set up her own secretarial services business when Windsor closed. Quite apart from administering my business, organising assignments and producing all my work on her word processor, she has acted as my counsellor. In the following pages I lay great emphasis on the need for those going through the trauma of losing their jobs – indeed all those who are job-hunting – to be able to talk things through with an independent counsellor. But I take this further and argue that everyone in business requires a totally trustworthy *alter ego* with whom to chew the fat. (Indeed, this is the basis of much of my consultancy work with the chairmen of medium-sized and private companies.) Pat's wise and enthusiastic support in that role has been invaluable.

David Mackintosh

1

The Pain Factor

'I would never read a book if it were possible to talk half an hour with the man who wrote it.'

PRESIDENT WOODROW WILSON

Learning the Rules

This book won't get you a good job – or any job at all come to that.

Only you can do that.

However, after nearly fifteen years in the recruitment game – as employer, recruitment consultant, outplacement counsellor and, yes, redundant executive and consequently candidate – it is just beginning to dawn on me that most people who set out to find a job do not really understand the world they are entering. It used to be said (may still be, for all I know) that there were three things no-one wants to hear: 'You're a lousy driver; you've no sense of humour; you're no good in bed.' To that I would add a fourth: 'You are about to start one of the most critical exercises in your life, finding a job, and you haven't got the faintest idea what you are up to.' You may not like to hear this, but how much better that you should accept it and learn the rules rather than flounder around helplessly, becoming more and more frustrated.

All the evidence suggests that, by understanding the market-place you are about to enter, you will improve the odds. I can't promise more than that, but that I can promise. For example, you see an advertisement which looks just right. You apply. You don't know this (though you can guess) – you are one of four hundred and fifty applicants. By following the precepts contained in this book you will increase substantially your chances of getting the job.

Naturally I would rather meet you face-to-face than write to you, so that we could adapt the general rules to your particular circumstances. But that is not possible. In the next chapter I place great stress on the need to find someone with whom you can discuss your campaign. That person is your counsellor, who will provide the listening ear and the other half of the debate, while this book will provide the know-how. The two together will provide the support you need.

I can't guarantee success, because the views of those involved in recruitment vary so much. Recruitment professionals – by which I mean personnel managers and recruitment consultants – are most unpredictable. They all do things differently and believe their methods are the only ones that work. Employers are in a sense worse, in that they all have their own foibles and prejudices which are hard to predict. (Although, as we shall see, with knowledge and cunning you may be able to circumvent these obstacles.)

An inevitable consequence of this diversity of opinion is that all other recruitment professionals will disagree with parts of what I have to say, in many cases violently. That's all to the good if you listen to what people tell you and then make up your own mind. As I say, it's your job and your life. Mind you, if anyone disagrees with certain fundamental rules you should ignore the advice.

For example, when I say that any basic CV (*curriculum vitae* or life history, or *résumé*, or personal profile, or what you will) longer than three sides of A4 paper should be burnt or shredded, that is a fact and you must ignore all other advice. I will produce some figures to justify this in my chapter on CVs. But my views on, say, the value of psychometric tests in recruitment or the desirability of replying to advertisements when you don't meet the specification *are* only my views, and many experienced recruiters would disagree. Then you must make up your own mind.

Executives – Actual and Aspiring

So who are you? Obviously you are looking for a job or thinking of doing so. For this book to be of much use you are either in, or aspiring to be in, the world of management or the professions. A suitable portmanteau word is 'executive', and I will use it in spite of the hackles it raises in some quarters.

If you are already an executive, you will almost certainly have been through the job-hunting process earlier in your life. But this may have been in very different circumstances from those you are in now. Perhaps the only time you have embarked on the process of seeking a job was when you left school or when you graduated. That may have been many years ago. The rules have, perhaps, changed more than you realise.

Alternatively you may now be on the threshold of your career. You may be about to graduate with your first degree or to obtain your master's. You may be completing a course which will make you professionally qualified. In this case your CV will be slim and you may feel that you have little to offer. Nonsense. You have a lot to offer and, if you read this book, you will be several jumps ahead of the competition.

Not every job-hunter has equally horrendous problems. There is a wide spectrum. I measure position in that spectrum by the Pain Factor, with a range of 1 to 10. Let us consider some examples.

The Pain Factor

Pain Factor 1   You are in a good job and your career is going well. You feel that it is time to make a change, particularly as there have been cutbacks in other similar companies and yours might be next, but you have little to worry about and can take your time. Of course, the situation may change for the worse with a concomitant increase in the Pain Factor, but for the moment you can relax.

Pain Factor 3   You are coming to the end of your university career. You will get a good degree in a marketable subject. You are thinking about your first job. Most new graduates with your qualifications find a suitable job. There is no reason why you should not do so, but you have read enough horror stories about unemployed graduates to feel mildly concerned. You have seen such headlines as 'New graduates facing tough hunt for jobs'... 'More graduates face dole queues'. You want to get your job-hunting skills tuned up.

Pain Factor 5   You have been working as an expatriate for the last five years and your contract is coming to an end. You are highly qualified and have useful experience, and are at a reasonably employable age – say thirty-eight – but you are finding that potential employers are not really interested in pursuing your application in view of the fact that you are three thousand miles from home and thus you would be expensive to bring back for interview. What to do?

Pain Factor 6   You are coming to the end of your university career. You will get a poor degree – just scraping through – in a subject unlikely to excite the milk-round. Those headlines about levels of unemployment for graduate job-hunters really worry you. You need to attack the job market from a position of knowledge.

Pain Factor 7   You are forty years old, well qualified with useful experience. Your company has been closed because of recession and the whole industry sector in which you are experienced is in decline. You really need to get back to work quickly and must think seriously about your options.

Pain Factor 9   You are fifty-two years old and have worked in the same company for thirty-six years. You are general manager of a subsidiary of a major plc based in a small market town in a rural area. Your company and the town are socially superimposed; you are the chairman of the company's sports club and also of the town's sports club (they share the same sports ground). Your social life and that of your family are intimately connected with those with whom you work and play. And then you are told that your services are no longer required. Things would be better, from your viewpoint, if the company was to be cut by, say, 30%, because then you could share the pain. But you are out on your own. You have the pressure of living in the environment which has rejected you — and you have not had to think about the recruitment market as a candidate for thirty-six years. Don't think that this is far-fetched: I have a specific case in mind and shall return to him later; his name is William Alexander.

Pain Factor 10   You are an Army major in an infantry battalion stationed in Germany. You are aged thirty-eight, have no academic or professional (other than purely military) qualifications beyond A-Level and you have three children at boarding school, largely paid for by the special allowance provided to prevent the constant changes of school. You and your family live in Army quarters, surrounded by your colleagues and their families, and you have to come home from a traumatic meeting with your commanding officer and tell your wife that you must leave the Army under the Options For Change policy. I give this case the maximum Pain Factor because it combines the parameters of employability (qualifications and experience), location and social pressures.

It is, of course, no help when you are under stress to learn that other people have greater problems than you. You may have a Pain Factor of only, say, 2 in global terms, but to you a problem is a problem. Last year I was introduced to Lauren, a university student with such a problem. She was reading business studies on a four-year course and had to find an industrial attachment for the third year. As it was by now late-August and nothing had materialised, life looked pretty bleak for her. We talked it through for a couple of hours and I am happy to say that a networking operation produced the answer — an interesting job close to home.

Worst Case Scenario

Recently I came across a new American verb – like so many American expressions it is grammatically appalling, yet brilliantly explicit. So I am confident that you will understand me when I say that I am going to 'worst-case-scenario' this book. I trust it will prove a real help to all those suffering from a high Pain Factor, but even if your problems are much, much less – and I hope they are – there is bound to be something here to help you in your search for that good job.

Terminology

One difficulty in looking at job-hunting from three different perspectives – recruiter, outplacement counsellor and candidate – is that it is easy to get in a muddle over terminology. For example, the outplacement industry employs a selection of descriptions for those who come for help. They are known, variously, as 'clients', 'candidates' and 'customers.' The first is particularly confusing, as the firms which pay outplacement counsellors to look after their cast-offs are variously known as 'clients' or 'sponsors'. So I am going to define seven terms that I will use throughout this book, which will enable me to switch from the recruitment world to the outplacement world without confusion:

a. **Recruitment**
(i)   The *Client* is the employer seeking to fill a vacancy who pays the recruiter to produce a short-list.
(ii)   The *Recruiter*, who produces the short-list, is either a recruitment consultant or a member of the client's personnel department.
(iii)   The *Candidate* is considered for the job. If he or she responds to an advertisement, the candidate is also, technically, an *Applicant* (unlike someone who is head-hunted, who isn't).

b. **Outplacement**
(i)   As will be seen, most outplacement is paid for by the unfortunate person's previous employer. The firm providing that benefit is known as the *Sponsor*.
(ii)   The *Counsellor* provides advice, expertise and probably administrative support. In most cases the counsellor works for an outplacement firm, but he/she may be an independent.
(iii)   This leaves a gap – what to call a person being counselled in the job-hunting process. I have already used up the popular – and

confusing — terms. So I will call the recipient of outplacement counselling the *Patient*. When I introduced this expression I was apprehensive, but to my surprise those whom I was counselling took to the title with enthusiasm.

Sex

The English language is somewhat inadequate in describing a person in a non-sexist fashion. I cannot subscribe to that appalling construction 'If anyone wants to check the spelling of a word, they should look it up in a dictionary', which muddles the singular and the plural. So I shall be relatively random in describing the players as 'him' or 'her'. The former will predominate, since in a recruitment operation seeking reasonably senior executives, male candidates outnumber female candidates by about 9:1. And a similar ratio applies when I look at the list of all the patients I have counselled. This imbalance is much less marked in the more creative and artistic industries such as publishing, advertising and television, and also when considering graduate recruitment.

As to sex discrimination, my thoughts on that are given in chapter 13.

Examples

Throughout this book, I cite examples to illustrate my points. There is some danger in arguing from the particular to the general (and one leaves oneself open to that word beloved of critics, 'anecdotal') but I believe such illustrations are helpful.

The maintenance of confidentiality must, of course, be paramount. So if I name a patient called Katie Evans who used to work for a furniture manufacturer in Yorkshire, I am probably actually referring to Steve Wigglesworth who was until recently a hotelier in South Wales. The message will be there but, as they used to say in *Dragnet*, 'only the names have been changed to protect the innocent'.

The First Principle of War

Finally, in this introductory chapter, let me introduce you to (or remind you of) the First Principle of War: *Selection and Maintenance of the Aim*. This, I suggest, should be your first principle in all you do in your search for that elusive good job. Take a simple example to which I will return. Ask yourself: 'What is the *aim* of a CV?' I always ask my patients this, and receive a variety of answers: 'To get a job', 'To describe myself' and so on. Rubbish. The simple and correct answer is: 'To get an interview', and your CV should therefore be written with that aim in mind.

To summarise:
* Only you can get that good job.
* You will improve dramatically your chances if you understand the job-hunting process.
* Some of the content of this book is controversial, and may not suit you. You must adopt your own style.
* This book covers the worst case. If you have a low Pain Factor and some knowledge of the job-hunting process, you will have to be selective.
* The illustrative examples are all essentially true, but names, places, etc. have been changed to preserve confidentiality.
* Before you embark on any action, determine your *aim*.

2

Dumping the Pain

*'I have striven not to laugh at human actions, not to weep at them,
nor to hate them, but to understand them.'*

SPINOZA

A Traumatic Experience

Much has been written by (typically) industrial psychologists about
the reactions of those who are made redundant or fired. If you want
to go into the subject in depth, you won't lack for material and
pretty good material it is too. I am bound to say that the industrial
psychologists I have come across are almost without exception sound
and helpful – thoroughly good eggs in fact.

But you want to get on with your job-hunting and don't have time
to read learned tomes on the subject. So I will start this chapter by
describing briefly the typical reaction to such traumatic events in order
to give you enough information for you to understand what is
happening to you when the axe falls.

Similarity with Death

In many ways, losing one's job is like losing a relation or friend
through death.

One way of losing your job is retirement at the age of sixty-five
after forty-three years with one company. (This is, of course, an
increasingly unlikely scenario today.) We can liken this to the death of
a loved ninety-three-year-old grandparent. You are sad and feel the
loss; there is a need to mourn – and also to give thanks for a happy
life and a peaceful death. Then your own life goes on. So it is with
normal retirement. Adjustment to the new *modus vivendi* will be
necessary, and there will be a feeling of loss – loss of colleagues,

of routine, of achievement at work. But this process – let's call it mourning – soon passes, and life in retirement takes on its own pattern.

The other end of the spectrum is far more traumatic. The death of, say, a young relative in an accident – particularly if the finger of blame can be pointed at a specific third party, such as a drunken driver. Then the reaction will be quite different and reasonably predictable.

And so it is with the unexpected loss of your job, particularly if you are in a position such that your prospects of re-employment appear to be marginal if not downright difficult. To those who have not been made redundant this comparison may seem fanciful, if not near blasphemous. But those who have been through the trauma will recognise the validity.

The Stages of Reaction

So what is your reaction likely to be when you suddenly lose your job? You will probably go through a number of stages.

To some extent the pattern of your reaction will depend on the competence of the person chosen to give you the bad news. In an ideal world your line manager, properly briefed and trained, should bite the bullet and do the dirty job. However, many line managers recoil from this task and hand it to the Human Resources (the modern jargon for Personnel) Department. I even know of cases where the actual news has been given by an outplacement counsellor – a major abrogation of responsibility by management. But, as we shall see, the key point is that the task of giving the bad news should be done professionally, so there is no doubt as to what has been said.

You may say that you have already been through the process and what follows is history. But I believe it will help you to come to terms with your new situation if you understand what you went through. On the other hand, if you are reading this book because you predict a disaster of this nature, you will be forewarned.

Shock

Your first reaction is shock. This will be relatively short-lived, but during that brief period you will hear and absorb nothing.

Disbelief

Then you reject the message: 'I don't believe it ... you're joking ... there must be some mistake.' Disbelief like this is a common reaction to bad news, such as the unexpected death I referred to above. This is where the deliverer of the news must get it right, and make it clear that the decision is irrevocable.

There is not a lot you can do about the way the news is given to you, but you must get over that disbelief stage. The danger is that the deliverer of the bad news may hold out some hope – probably out of misdirected kindness – of the variety: 'Of course, things may change, nothing is final until it has happened.'

This is very dangerous. I recall one patient – Alistair Mackay – who was given a false hope to cling to. He was general manager of a subsidiary company and his parent group sold the company to a competitor. The new owners said they would close Alistair's site in six months' time and asked him to stay for that period to manage the closure. To encourage him to agree they hinted – entirely spuriously – that this just might lead to a long-term job in the group. That potential life-line was all Alistair needed, and he did not start any form of job-hunting, in spite of being both encouraged and bullied, until the six months came to an end. Instead, he sat in the kitchen with his wife and they whinged together. What a waste of time.

Rage

Following acceptance of reality – a process which may take minutes or weeks – comes rage or anger. Lots of it.

A remarkable example of anger publicly expressed comes in Lee Iacocca's autobiography. You will probably recall that he rose to become President of the Ford Motor Company only to be fired by Henry Ford after eight years at the top. Subsequently he wrote his autobiography, *Iacocca*, in which he described in considerable detail his departure from Ford and the pain and rage it caused. His book shows very clearly how deep those scars were and how lasting his rage: 'For me, the pain continued long after the deed was done'. The whole of the chapters entitled 'The Showdown' and 'The Day After' demonstrate that Iacocca's rage at Henry Ford is there for ever.

This anger may be reinforced by action additional to the simple dismissal. Iacocca tells of how he was, under the terms of his 'resignation', given the use of an office until he had found a new job. He describes it as 'Little more than a cubicle with a small desk and telephone ... in an obscure warehouse'. He continues: 'This final humiliation was much worse than being fired. It was enough to make me want to kill – I wasn't quite sure who, Henry Ford or myself. Murder or suicide were never real possibilities, but I did start to drink a little more – and shake a lot more. I really felt I was coming apart at the seams.'

The anger will be there whether you are on your own, which probably means you have been fired, or are one of a group, as happens when a whole company or site is closed. In the latter case you can collectively blame 'them up there' (though there is more pleasure to be had if you can identify one culpable individual).

This is a healthy and proper reaction and you should let go – you are dumping the pain. Don't let go completely by physically attacking the object of your rage – riding into town with a six-gun went out with John Wayne – but the person delivering the bad news should know enough to let you give vent to your feelings in no uncertain way.

Despair

Once your rage has subsided you will go into some level of despair. The depth of this despair will depend on your personality and circumstances. In some cases this stage can lead to clinical depression. Clearly it is not my job to diagnose your depth of despair and to say whether or not it should be classed as clinical depression. But I would say that depression is not a disgrace and can be treated. So if you do go into what I call (from personal experience) that black downwards vortex – either at this stage or at any stage of your job-hunt – go and see your GP. In the short-lived despair phase, however, it should be possible, with help, to switch from such attitudes as 'What shall I do? ... How will I face the world? ... What a waste my life has been' to the 'OK, let's do something about this' mode. We will call this stage Rebuilding.

Being Mugged

A vivid description of being on the receiving end of the firing process was given by Virginia Ironside in *The Times* in December 1992. She had been the agony aunt of the *Sunday Mirror* and was fired so that Marje Proops, who was agony aunt for the *Daily Mirror*, could do the same job for the *Sunday Mirror*. Ironside wrote: 'It is like being mugged. I sit at home feeling faint and dizzy and shocked ... Everyone tells me things will work out fine ... But until you have a job you're just another unemployed person, sitting at home and feeling as if you're floating in outer space.' But she concluded on an optimistic note: 'Maybe I'll be able to look back on this grim Christmas and see the incident as a challenge, a gift. And that I have not so much lost a job as gained a future. I hope so.' Rebuilding had begun.

After reading that remarkable piece I wrote to her asking if I could quote her words here. She was kind enough to phone me and added a most interesting postscript. By that time she had found another job and become agony aunt of *Today* newspaper. But although she was delighted with her new job, the pain of being fired was as strong as ever.

My point in telling you all this is to reassure you that you are in no sense abnormal if you still have that feeling of being mugged even after finding a new job. For the moment, however, you must put aside your rage when you start to look for your next job, or you will never achieve your aim.

Rebuilding

So you must start to rebuild and to take control of your own life. Of course it's difficult, but inactivity will achieve nothing. Taking control of your own future may be a particularly difficult thing to do when you are young and the world seems to be against you, but you must get on top of the situation. Listen to Margaret Wallis (Director, University of Warwick Career Advisory Services) talking to the *Daily Telegraph* (February 1993) on behalf of the Association of Graduate Careers Advisory Services: 'This year's graduates are going to face difficulties, but many are adopting a defeatist attitude. They just think it is not even worth trying. But you won't get a job if you don't apply.'

In saying you need determination to solve the problem I am not, however, advocating precipitate action. There are certain things you should *not* do immediately.

Don't Think You Are Cursed

There is no stigma in redundancy. You must get right out of your head any idea that you are an untouchable in polite society, and unemployable from the work viewpoint, because you suddenly find yourself out of work.

I am not sure I could have written that paragraph in such uncompromising terms fifteen (indeed ten) years ago, but today there is no longer any disgrace. This is not just me speaking. There have been surveys about this, and it is not uncommon to read statements that 90% of personnel people do not view redundant candidates adversely. Indeed, there will be occasions when it is positively an advantage for you to be out of work, so that you can join your new employer immediately.

You can and must discard your natural feeling of inadequacy, and look the world squarely in the eyes.

Don't Panic

Once you are over the shock, you will want to take positive action as soon as possible. But there are risks in moving too quickly, because you will probably make mistakes which you may find difficult to unravel.

Typically this will involve phoning or writing to a large number of friends, ex-colleagues and useful contacts – and almost certainly giving them a confused message which doesn't give them a chance to help, but merely to sympathise. I made this mistake when my job at 3i suddenly evaporated. Fortunately one of the first people I wrote to was a wise man with his feet firmly on the ground who wrote back to me saying that he would be delighted to help but, until he had some clearer idea of what I wanted him to do, there wasn't much he could do or say. This brought me up short and caused me to reflect a little before going further. I return to this question of preparation before action in the chapter on networking.

Don't Write your CV

The other typical reaction is to produce a CV in a hurry and distribute it widely. Inevitably it won't be a very good CV and you then have the wrong document with the wrong message in the wrong hands.

Most CVs written in haste are rubbish. Writing your CV is eight chapters ahead. By all means think about yourself, your career, your relationships, your hopes and dreams. You can even start to write your autobiography. But leave it at that for the moment, please.

Do You Tell your Spouse or Partner?

The answer to this question seems obvious, but not everyone does the sensible thing. I am sure that you have read reports of redundant executives who have set off for work each morning wearing a suit and briefcase in hand, spent the day in the library, at the cinema or wherever and returned in time for supper – and this has continued for weeks. You can imagine the effect this has on the wife (it is usually men who are so foolish as to keep such things to themselves) when eventually the truth is unearthed. So the answer to the above question must surely be 'Yes' and you must tell the whole story. There will be some cases where doing so will add additional major burdens, and I pray that you are not one of them.

Who Else Should Get the Whole Story?

Now it's becoming difficult. There are pitfalls ahead and it is time to talk about counselling and other forms of help.

To summarise:
* Disbelief, shock, anger and a modicum of despair are natural reactions to losing your job – you are not alone in your response.
* If you are genuinely depressed, see your GP. Depression is nothing to be ashamed of.
* Being without a job is no disgrace.
* Don't panic. Hit the market only when you're ready.
* Don't put out a hurried and inadequate CV.
* Tell your spouse or partner the truth as soon as possible.

3

Counselling and Others Sources of Help

'There are no words to express the abyss between isolation and having one ally. It may be conceded to the mathematician that four is twice two but two is not twice one; two is two thousand times one.'

G.K. CHESTERTON

The Need

I now want to discuss the whole issue of counselling. The concept of counselling is not new to you, although you may have used different words to describe the process. My thesaurus includes several synonyms for 'counsellor', such as 'adviser', 'coach', 'mentor', 'guide', 'guru' and 'tutor'. (In the Gunners we have a saying, 'An officer is as good as his first battery commander' — a mentor concept that can be extended to any hierarchical community.) But we will stick to 'counsellor' in this context.

My argument here is very simple. You need someone to talk to, to listen to, to debate with; someone, in short, with whom to share your hopes, fears and dreams.

'Stop,' you say, 'but I have already got such a person in my spouse.' Well, yes and no. I am all in favour of your confiding in your partner up to a point, but only up to a point. Suppose that you are the household's major breadwinner. Your loss of income is serious. 'Should we sell the house immediately and move into something smaller?' will inevitably be asked. (The answer is, almost certainly, 'No'.) So if you are feeling low, it is going to damage morale on the home front if you try to dump that concern on to your partner. Far better to take your worries to a counsellor who should therefore, by definition, not be too close to you. So we deduce that you need to find a counsellor who will act responsibly and confidentially and who, ideally, understands the job scene. However, your counsellor's knowledge of job-hunting is far less important than his or her listening, debating and supporting skills; you can acquire the knowledge from this book.

Do not, however, expect your counsellor to do the work for you. In golfing parlance, your counsellor is your caddy rather than your foursomes partner.

Life Support Systems

The deficiencies of your new lifestyle are only beginning to dawn. Quite apart from major matters, such as paying your mortgage and returning your company car, if you have one, you are now devoid of your own corporate identity. Where is your office, your desk, your telephone? Who is going to type your letters and answer the phone? Why, you haven't even got a business card.

Major Outplacement Firms

If you are lucky, both these problems — the need for counselling and the lack of life-support systems — will be solved when your previous employer offers you outplacement counselling with a major outplacement firm.

I will not list these firms here, lest any I fail to mention should sue me. Most of the good major firms will accept only patients sent by corporate sponsors (this is in their Code of Conduct). Your sponsor (i.e. your previous employer) may send you to a specific firm or, alternatively, may give you a choice from a list of two or three.

Most outplacement firms usually have a head office in London and a number of regional offices. Each office has, in addition to the consulting staff, work stations with telephones and possibly PCs, backed by research and secretarial facilities, a closed circuit TV (CCTV) studio and a variety of specialist skills to call upon.

The concept is that you 'go to work' at the office. To some people this merely provides distraction and an excuse to gossip. But in most cases the routine and the sense of purpose are highly beneficial; the alternative of working at home in a vacuum can be very depressing and counter-productive. When I worked in an outplacement consultancy in Bristol some time ago, one of my patients said that the routine of coming in to the office every day made all the difference to coping with redundancy. This was by no means untypical.

So I support the use of this type of organisation if you are offered the service. But never forget that you are, indirectly at least, the customer, and are entitled to ensure you receive the service you need. I suggest that you insist on two things:

1. A firm with an office near to your home, as travelling seems very expensive in the absence of a salary (and perhaps the loss of a company car). If this is not possible, ensure your counsellor will give you a decent chunk of time when you do make the journey, which will be less frequently than in the case of other patients who live close to the office. Many counsellors deal in one-and-a-half-hour slots – up to five a day. If you have a long way to travel, that is not good enough. In any event, there is a case for longer sessions to give the patient and the counsellor every opportunity to get to know each other. I prefer to work in six-hour slots with a pub lunch for a breather. This sort of programme allows, for example, a lengthy CCTV interview, a chance to watch the whole thing and then have a repeat performance. The patient can then (if so desired!) take the video cassette home and demonstrate progress to the family. All this in addition to the normal update on activities, analysis of success/failure since the last meeting, and the action plan.

2. The right to approve the selection of your counsellor. I know that we all recruit in our own image, so I admit to bias here, but I believe that your counsellor should have four characteristics:
   - Empathy with you, together with the necessary capacity for encouraging and/or bullying.
   - Some experience of the recruitment world as either a recruitment consultant or a Human Resources professional.
   - Experience of being made redundant.
   - Willingness to give you his/her home phone number.

   The last of these may be resisted, but don't weaken. There are bound to be occasions when you need to pick your guru's brains – e.g. in the evening before a morning interview which has been planned at short notice.

Ask for Help

If your employer does not offer you outplacement assistance, then ask for it. If nothing else, it will be a useful first exercise in asking for help during your job-hunting operation. Exactly what selling points you use will depend on the circumstances. You can always argue that morale amongst those employees who remain will be higher if they know that you have been helped – after all, they may be next. You can strengthen this argument if the social and working environments are superimposed – remember William Alexander with Pain Factor 9? In his case he could have argued that his continued presence in the community, while unemployed, would have been bad for everyone. Since outplacement counselling unquestionably reduces the time spent out of work (we can argue about how much, but not about the basic premise) the argument is powerful and should result in some help in many cases. It is, however, expensive if one is given the full executive treatment (typically 15% of salary plus £1,000) and you may have to do a deal for a reduced service.

Smaller Firms and Sole Traders

If your previous employer agrees to pay for outplacement counselling, you may have to source it for yourself. You could consider a major firm or you may prefer – particularly if there isn't one with an office near your home – to find a counsellor in your area. There are lots of small firms and individuals working in this field. Be careful: the best are excellent; the worst are charlatans. A small operation will not be able to provide the level of life-support systems you will obtain from a major firm. On the other hand, your counsellor will probably see you more as an individual than as a statistic on the monthly report.

It should also go without saying that you must check on any counsellor you are planning to use. The best way to find someone is by personal recommendation from a person whose judgement you respect. Indeed, the search for a counsellor may be a useful excuse for some early networking, about which you will learn more in chapter 12.

Your tax position on the fee paid by a sponsor for outplacement, may be complex. I cannot give financial advice here – I am not qualified to do so and the position appears to change from time to time. This is unquestionably an area where professional advice is necessary – preferably at no cost to you, if it is given by your sponsor's finance director or auditors.

One final point on the relationship between the sponsor, the patient and the counsellor. The whole outplacement process is strange in that the fees are paid by the sponsor, yet all the professional care is directed at the patient. You may, therefore, feel that the counsellor has a dual loyalty and may even give advice which is in the sponsor's, rather than the patient's, interests.

If you have an outplacement firm, or an individual counsellor, of integrity, this need not worry you. If it does, discuss it with your counsellor, who may not realise your concern. Certainly I made this mistake when I was counselling Isobel Tomlinson, the fees having been paid by her sponsor company – chairman Bill Scott. It was only afterwards, when she wrote to me, that I realised this had worried her. One paragraph of her letter read:

> It was certainly a great relief getting back to work after my enforced 'rest' and I offer you my sincere thanks for the help you provided. I must admit to being a little suspicious of your motives, expecting you to steer me in a direction specified by Bill (after all, he was paying your not inconsiderable fee) but after the first week or so, it became clear that your own integrity would not allow such things to influence you.

Which is all very well, but if I had done the job properly, I would have identified this fear earlier and allayed it immediately.

Going It Alone

If you cannot persuade your employer to provide help, you must decide whether or not to pay someone out of your own suddenly diminished pocket. Whilst doing so might be the right move in the long run, my advice is that you should at all costs avoid making a hasty decision. You are at your most vulnerable immediately after you have received the bad news and you should be very careful before taking on additional financial commitments. This is not to say that a degree of professional counselling may not be highly cost effective for you in your present circumstances, but do take your time, check out any counsellor thoroughly and establish very early on the payment ceiling and what you will get for that sum of money.

Better still, use an experienced friend as your counsellor – perhaps someone who has retired and would be glad to talk things over with you on a regular basis, thus adding a little spice to retired life (and perhaps finding an excuse not to go shopping – again – and not to dig the garden in the rain). Don't be backward about asking for help; people who are asked feel flattered and wanted, and rarely say no. Indeed, this is a cornerstone of the networking concept.

Do not worry if your personally recruited counsellor lacks expertise in the field. This book will provide that. What you need is that ally to whom G.K. Chesterton refers in the quotation at the head of this chapter.

Other Sources of Help

Apart from commercial outplacement consultancies there are many organisations available to help you. Inevitably you will find some less useful — often a lot less useful — than others. The value of such an organisation is just as likely to depend on local individuals as it is on the structure within which it operates. So you must try them all. Some can help only if you have been out of work for a specific period of time, some only if your savings are below a certain threshold, and so on.

Don't feel embarrassed about asking for help. You probably read of a case discussed excitedly in the papers (December 1992) of a redundant insurance salesman who had been earning £400,000 per annum and had lost his job. His mortgage of something approaching £2,000 per month was being paid for from taxpayers' (i.e. our) money. It is not for me to comment here on the way in which your money and mine should be spent. The fact is that help is available in certain circumstances (although help as extreme as this is being curtailed) and your job is to find it and make use of it. You owe a little self-interest to yourself and your family.

Help Available in Getting Back to Work

Citizens Advice Bureau (CAB) The starting point. The service is free and there is a stock of pamphlets on most subjects. You will find your nearest CAB in the telephone directory.

Training and Enterprise Councils (TECs) (England and Wales) TECs have a particular interest in people who plan to go into business for themselves or become self-employed. With the growth of unemployment they have become increasingly concerned with relevant aspects of training, including training in job-hunting and retraining in skills. TECs vary in style and competence — the good ones are excellent and we'll leave it at that. See your telephone directory.

Local Enterprise Councils (LECs) LECs are the Scottish equivalent of TECs.

Training and Employment Agency Equivalent to TECs/LECs in Northern Ireland.

Employment Services (ES) The Employment Department has several schemes to help people get back to work. Most of the schemes are available only to those who have been out of work for six months or more, but sometimes you can get help more quickly. Services vary — job clubs, seminars on job-hunting, updating of skills, etc. Either look for Employment Services in the telephone book or get details from the CAB.

Chambers of Commerce These vary tremendously from place to place. It is certainly worthwhile for you to contact your local chamber. If you can get there by networking, so much the better.

Other Sources of Help There are many. For example, local universities and colleges may run courses which are relevant to you. Self-help groups run job clubs. You will find them easy to track down if you enquire from your local CAB, TEC/LEC, ES or, indeed, library. In certain cases grants and/or loans are available and these bodies will be able to advise you.

Specific Advice

If you need advice on a specific matter, such as your entitlement to redundancy payments, there are many organisations to which you can refer. The best place to start is the CAB, who will be able to point you at the appropriate organisation to deal with your specific problem.

When drafting this chapter, I was fortunate enough to come across a booklet published by the BBC. It was edited for BBC Education by Liz Barclay and was initially published as *Work it Out* by Radio 5 and later as *Work it through* by Radio 2. The BBC has kindly agreed to let me reproduce the complete list, thus saving me hours of laborious research. The list is at appendix 1 and is, to the best of my knowledge, accurate at the time of going to press — though things do change. Any errors are my fault rather than the BBC's.

Appendix 1 also includes a few additional details which you may find helpful.

Enjoy

Now you have to start on the search for that elusive job, preferably with the support of a counsellor, however obtained. You will find it hard going, but the whole process could actually be fun as you pit your wits against the obstacles. Yes, I really do mean that your job-hunting operation can be a stimulating and enjoyable process if you enter into it in the right spirit. And the fact that you are enthusiastic and dynamic will communicate itself during the many meetings and interviews you are going to have.

But first you must decide who you are and what you want to do in future. And that takes us to the next chapter.

To summarise:

* If you are offered professional outplacement consultancy by your previous employer, take it. But remember that you are the customer – make sure you get what you need.
* Get a counsellor. This need not necessarily be an expensive professional – a trusted friend will be of great value.
* If you do pay for counselling yourself, check out the counsellor before you pay him any money. Anyone who is any good will be happy to provide references.
* Make use of the various organisations that are there to help you.
* Face up to your job-hunt with enthusiasm. It could be one of the most exciting and enjoyable periods of your life.

4

Are You Who You Think You Are?

'Neddy Seagoon: *Yes, but who are you?*
Famous Eccles: *Oh, the hard ones first, eh?'*
THE LAST GOON SHOW

Keep an Open Mind

The initial reaction of someone who is made redundant is, typically, to embark immediately on the search for an identical job. There is a certain logic in this — particularly for an experienced executive. If, for example, you have spent the last twenty-five years manufacturing textiles, you have something to offer a textile manufacturer. And you are likely to appeal to one, since many employers are interested primarily in what candidates have done in the past rather than what they are capable of doing in the future.

However, even if you are a specialist, it would be wise to take a few moments to consider the various options. And for someone embarking on a career for the first time (e.g. a school-leaver or a new graduate) or someone who has to make a major change (e.g. leaving the forces or returning to work after raising a family) a fundamental assessment is essential.

Why Work at All?

The first question you must ask yourself is 'Why work at all?' Some people are shocked when I ask them that. But why? There is no scientific law saying that every adult human being between the ages of six and sixty should either be undergoing education or be gainfully employed. The answer is usually 'because I need the money', and one can't argue with that. But then the next question follows logically: 'Do you need to earn anything like as much money as you have earned before?' By rigorously examining the financial aspects of your future life you may be able to come up with some surprising answers.

So when it comes to assessing your options, there is initially a case for being very open minded. Not everyone would agree. There are two schools of thought.

Sniper's Rifle

First, there is the focused school, which I call the 'sniper's rifle approach'. This is the 'I've always wanted to be a doctor' syndrome. We had a chap at school like this. A brilliant linguist who could barely add, he was determined to become a civil engineer and build bridges, roads and railways. This he achieved by dedicated hard work. Presumably he also learnt to add, since his bridges didn't collapse.

The sniper's rifle approach demands, initially, a very detailed analysis of your capabilities, characteristics and interests – the 'know thyself' process which I loosely call psychometrics (discussed at length later in this chapter).

For people beginning their careers there may be some purpose in detailed analysis of this nature. But the analytical approach seems to me to be restrictive, in that it eliminates options rather than creates them. There are, however, many who are convinced that the focused approach achieves the best results. In particular, the professional outplacement world seems to favour it and produces statistics which claim that highly focused job searches are correspondingly more effective than unfocused ones. It sometimes crosses my cynical mind that outplacement firms take this view because it adds a mystical dimension to the job-hunting process and, perhaps, even justifies the fees.

Anyway, Eccles is quite right. 'Who are you?' is a very difficult question to answer.

The Shotgun

My view is much more pragmatic. I believe that most of us, unlike my engineering-orientated former fellow pupil, drift into our working life rather than direct ourselves into it. When I was born, the midwife didn't say to my mother, 'Mrs Mackintosh, you've got a fine little boy who will go into the Army for National Service and enjoy it so much that he will stay in it for twenty-seven years and then will be lucky enough to be employed as a management consultant and . . .' Of course she didn't.

Examine your past. I suspect that a number of uncontrolled events – a gifted teacher in a particular subject, a sibling you wanted to be different from, a place at university in your second-choice subject, the particular interests of your partner – the list is endless – have been the deciding factors in who you are now. So your task is not to exclude possibilities by adopting a highly focused posture, but to open your mind and to see what the world has to offer. The shotgun approach.

The Rest of Your Life Starts Now

I want you to consider your future as one of lots of possibilities, all of which you would like to explore. Certainly you will not be able to explore them all – time and money will preclude that – but don't close your mind at the outset. Remember, the rest of your life starts now.

Living in a Rotunda

Imagine that you are sitting in a swivel chair in the centre of the floor of a rotunda (this is a room with one continuous curved wall, like the inside of a drum). The wall is full of doors which you look at as you swing around in your chair. If you are lucky, one or two doors may already be ajar. Most are shut, shut and locked even; some may be welded shut. Each door represents an opportunity.

The doors are painted a variety of colours. Most are, say, brown, representing jobs in the field for which your education, training and experience most naturally fit you. Others are green (consultancy perhaps), blue (teaching), yellow (a change of discipline), red (starting your own business), black (locum management) and so on. Some have a diagonal white stripe, indicating contract work overseas.

Now your job is to open as many of those doors as you can. Remember, you cannot make a decision whether or not to step through the door until it is open. Or, to put it more explicitly, you cannot reject a job until it has been offered to you.

Unfortunately, the doors have a characteristic which makes life difficult. Once a door is open it starts to swing shut. Some doors close very quickly, while others remain open long enough for you to have a good look. You must aim to open several doors at the same time, so that you have a choice of which doorway to enter. Timing is very important if you are to have a choice. (Though I am bound to say that these days choice may not be your top priority.)

As I have said, you may – all right, will – have to ignore some of these doors because you haven't got the time to push at them all. Job-hunting – I hope you've got this message by now – is a full-time job. But never lose sight of the truth that you cannot reject an offer until that offer is made.

As I write this I can hear experts in the job-hunting business jumping up and down shouting, 'The man's mad — it's a muddle', and up to a point they are right. The danger of the approach I propose is that other people will be confused by your lack of focus. So don't confuse them. You will discuss these ideas with your counsellor and, provided that doing so won't cause worry, your spouse. But to others you will give a clear picture. So, if you respond to an advertisement for a job as European sales director, don't tell the interviewer that you are also thinking of teaching in business schools. But that doesn't stop you talking to the business schools.

All this may sound fanciful, but it's not. Recently a patient of mine, an accountant with excellent experience as finance director in a quality company, was at a networking meeting and a door marked 'Personnel' swung open — he hardly had to push it. He looked through the doorway, liked what he saw and stepped through. He is now European personnel director of a major multinational company, doing a super job and loving every minute of it. If he had taken the highly focused approach, he would not, I suggest, have noticed the door beginning to open and would have rejected all thought of looking through the doorway. And this wasn't a question of taking a lousy job and the easy way out; it is a fascinating appointment, very well paid and an excellent career move.

The same arguments apply if you are starting or restarting your career. Do not limit your options. I accept that it is not easy in that the young are expected to specialise early. Today if, for example, you want to become a lawyer, you are encouraged to read law at university. (In former times you read mediaeval history, classics or whatever, and then started on law after graduating.) So your room for manoeuvre is restricted, but, I beg you, keep the options open.

Retraining Options

One option is to increase your skills and/or qualifications (not necessarily the same thing) before going out into the job market. You might consider general training, e.g. for an MBA (Master of Business Administration) or a DMS (Diploma in Management Studies). These are major undertakings if studied on full-time residential courses, and you will have to consider carefully the financial implications. Such degrees can also be taken by part-time study over a longer period, but that method is unlikely to be of much use to you in your present predicament. For access to higher education apply to your county education authority, but you will almost certainly find that strict means testing will apply.

If you are interested in an MBA, you may find it useful to see a recent edition of *The MBA Career Guide*. You can obtain single editions direct (details at appendix 1), but they cost money – your friendly local library should be able to help.

There are also shorter courses which can give you an additional or enhanced skill which is marketable. You may be able to do a deal, so that your previous employer pays. When I left 3i, I traded the cost of outplacement consultancy (I thought I knew enough about job-hunting) for two weeks of courses qualifying me to administer aptitude tests and personality questionnaires.

An obvious possibility here is languages. I am looking at a headline as I write: 'One in four companies hit by lack of language skills'. Is your skill in any language (or, better still, languages) sufficient that you could become fluent after a fortnight's or a month's total immersion course? If so, this would be well worth considering.

Changing Direction

Should you change direction completely? Perhaps you might qualify as a teacher. Or perhaps you might work overseas. The right experience plus the right skills plus right personality could put you in demand in the former Soviet bloc (and particularly Eastern Europe) and the Third World. The British Executive Service Overseas (Beso) might be worth talking to (details at appendix 1). This is a substantial organisation backed by the Ministry for Overseas Development, the CBI and the IOD.

Overseas contract work for commercial/industrial companies can be lucrative – though the money is usually hard earned. You should be able to identify appropriate companies (and also recruitment consultancies handling this sort of appointment) through advertisements in the general and specialised press, and also by networking.

Another aspect of contract work is the short-term locum (or temporary) management assignment. You would probably be unwise to take on a poorly-paid assignment just to get back to work in order to restore your morale. Nevertheless, opportunities do occur, particularly for the older executive who can bring experience to a faltering organisation. This could be a stepping stone to a permanent job or to a non-executive directorship, a topic I shall return to when discussing prejudice based on age (chapter 13).

Then there is self-employed consultancy. Lots of people make a good living as such; many more don't. My view is that you need either consultancy experience or freedom from excessive financial pressure, or both (e.g. the children have left home and you have a subsistence level pension) before becoming self-employed, but there are many who could prove me wrong.

Perhaps you are a frustrated entrepreneur and should start your own business. This is an entire subject on its own and I don't want to get diverted here. The downside is that most new businesses fail (a large percentage). The positive message is that lots of people are enjoying a thoroughly satisfactory life doing their own thing. So don't be put off if you really think you can make it. You can get advice and help from several sources: The CAB, the TEC, the Chamber of Commerce and the Federation of Small Businesses (see appendix 1).

Working for Less Money

If you are financially secure, should you consider working for less money – or even none at all – and putting something back into society whilst keeping busy? Plenty of charities would love to use your skills. You may well not be in this fortunate position and the point may not be relevant to you, but all I ask is that you should consider all the options.

Helping You to Decide

In deciding where to direct your further energies you will naturally consult various people – your spouse, your counsellor and anyone else with a useful input. You will, quite possibly, come across more esoteric methods to help you decide who you are and what you're good at. We will now discuss them.

Psychometrics

It is highly probable that you will, at some stage, be exposed to the world of assessment tests. We will see in a moment that 'tests' is an inadequate title to give them, and I will use the general term 'psychometrics' to cover the whole spectrum.

You should know what they involve. In your job-hunt you may come across them in one or both of two ways. First, as part of the 'getting to know yourself' process. Secondly, as part of the recruitment process which potential employers use to assess you, the candidate. How much use they are in either role is arguable, but that should not prevent your knowing about them.

Know Thyself

In the 'getting to know thyself' mode, psychometrics are frequently used in the early stages of outplacement. The trouble is, it seems to me, that if the personality profile is what you expect, you say, 'Well, that's very accurate, but so what?' And, if the profile is not what you expect, you say, 'What nonsense, it doesn't work.'

There is another drawback. If the profile system works, it should produce the same answer each time – for surely someone's underlying personality does not change from day to day. Well, mine certainly did when I did masses of these questionnaires during the psychometrics courses referred to above. Was I, I wondered, a freak? Thus it was a great relief (in one sense only) to learn subsequently that clinical psychologists in the NHS were being overwhelmed by people 'suffering mental stress caused by unemployment and the threat of redundancy ... the psychological state of unemployed people ... the scale of the problem quite horrendous ...' and so on. If things are that bad, surely one's psychological/personality profile is reactive to circumstances. All of which strikes me as making profiling at this stressful moment in your life somewhat suspect.

However, most of the people exposed to this process seem to enjoy it and approve of it, and therefore we must accept that I am wrong. Or is it just that we all like talking about ourselves?

Assessing Candidates

Moving on to the use of psychometrics in the assessment of candidates during recruitment, the position is more complex. With large organisations recruiting hundreds of school-leavers or graduates annually, there should be a large enough population on which to base preferred personality traits. With smaller companies, however, I wonder whether they know what they want in terms of personality. I often claim, whilst recruiting executives for medium-sized and private companies, that I am acting in a Cilla Black mode. The process of matching people is complex, with luck playing a considerable part. When we come to discuss the recruitment process you will see that defining the ideal candidate is difficult and often depends on a number of unpredictable and indirect factors, which almost certainly would not be responsive to psychometrics.

But what are psychometrics? They are best split into tests, questionnaires and hybrids.

Aptitude Tests

The first group comprises genuine tests that have correct answers. Provided the test has previously been administered to an acceptably (in statistical terms) large number of people, it is possible to compare your performance with all those who have been tested in the past.

IQ (Intelligence Quotient) tests are aptitude tests within this definition. Provided one uses a properly validated test (a highly complex statistical process) it is possible to state someone's IQ and where that IQ fits into the spectrum of IQs of people of, say, a similar age group. Theoretically a pure IQ test produces pure gradings, but we are all realistic enough to know that practice improves the result. Aptitude tests encountered in assessment for jobs are likely to be more specific. For example they may refer to verbal or numerical reasoning. In the assessment of candidates for apprenticeships they probably include mechanical aptitude and spatial reasoning.

These tests must be accurately administered and strictly timed. The resulting score is then compared with statistical tables derived from the particular group being studied. For example, a score in a verbal reasoning test of 53 (in itself a totally meaningless figure) might indicate that the candidate is a 65 percentile against a population of new graduates testing for trainee manager jobs, but a 95 percentile for school-leavers applying for apprenticeships.

What does 'percentile' mean in this context? It says that in the first case the candidate is better at verbal reasoning than 65% of a population of graduates who have taken this particular test (and conversely, worse than the other 35%). In the second case, that the candidate is better than 95% of the group of potential apprentice school-leavers who have taken the test (and conversely, worse than 5%). In short, one aspires to score a high percentile.

I emphasise that this variety of test has the right answer. Occasionally one encounters so-called IQ tests which are nothing of the sort. For example, one fairly well-known organisation published an 'IQ test' which asked children to select the odd one out from run, walk, swim, dance. Clearly there is no right answer and I have tried it on many people to prove the point. Answers vary: 'walk – it is the only natural one'; 'swim –the rest take place on land'; 'swim – it is the only one in which you are horizontal to the medium'; 'swim – your feet don't touch the ground'; 'dance – with the rest you can have a race, an Olympic gold medal indeed'; 'dance – you don't go anywhere' and 'dance – it is the only one in which the movements are artificial' (this last from an occupational psychologist). Which answer is right? Obviously they all are; the answers tell you much more about how someone thinks than about innate intelligence.

Personality Questionnaires

This brings us conveniently to the second group, that of personality questionnaires. There is a wide variety of these. They invite the victim to answer questions to which there is no right or wrong answer. You might be asked, for example, whether you would rather go to a quiet dinner party for six or to a wild all-night party. Or – and this can become very esoteric – which words you like most and least from wool, water, computer, cricket (you will appreciate that I can't give actual examples for reasons of copyright). These questionnaires may be very long (more than a hundred questions is not untypical) and the process is not timed. At the end of it all you will be told whether you are an extrovert or an introvert, decisive or indecisive, a potential managing director or sales director, and so on. Some questionnaires deal with your interests rather than your personality. They will determine, for example, whether you are mechanically or artistically orientated. I have lumped interest questionnaires in with personality questionnaires for simplicity, but there is a vast library on the whole subject if you wish to pursue it.

The argument runs that all this information can help you to decide what you should do in the future. This view may be useful in helping a school-leaver or a graduate to select a career, but I cannot believe that this type of analysis really helps a mature executive to focus effectively on the future. The description of a personality may be accurate, but I am not convinced that the description can be turned into useful action.

Surprisingly to me, many outplacement patients say they find considerable value in psychometrics. I suspect that there are two reasons for this. First, at a time when your self-confidence is low, it is reassuring to have lots of people focusing on you and you alone. Secondly, in a properly run outplacement consultancy the feedback is given personally by the resident occupational psychologist (a profession for which I have great admiration). That is very important. This personality stuff is, in my opinion, extremely dangerous in the wrong hands. Indeed, at the end of my week's course on personality question-naires I declined a licence because I thought it wrong that someone unqualified (and a week's course could not be described in any sensible forum as a qualification in this field) should be allowed to undertake such work.

My point about personality work being dangerous in the wrong hands was illustrated by a friend of my daughter – we'll call her Sarah. After about two years in her first job following graduation, Sarah applied for a job and was subjected to a battery of tests and question-naires by some half-baked personnel person who was not a qualified psychologist. At the end of the process Sarah was told that she lacked leadership potential and was therefore unsuitable for the job in question. Naturally this news caused temporary loss of confidence, but being a Good Egg she pressed on with her search for a suitable career move and is now, eight years later, running a department of over twenty staff with immense skill. I don't know, but I imagine that the personnel person is still sitting at his desk doing the same kind of damage.

However, in qualified hands the whole business of analysing personality is probably harmless and may actually be useful.

Fringe Methods

Dabbling with the mysteries of personality doesn't stop there. Other methods of assessing personality come into fashion from time to time – some to stay, some to be consigned to history. I suppose that the ducking of witches was a form of personality test. The more popular one today, however, is graphology. In some countries this is very popular. In a most amusing and enlightening piece about France in *The Times*, Charles Bremner neatly nailed down graphology's coffin:

> 'France consumes more tranquillisers than any other nation. Surely, it is said, only irrational fear could be driving the craze for the supernatural on television and the recourse of senior businessmen to astrology and graphology.'

Should you come across graphology, you must judge its efficacy for yourself. I will only say that I was very keen on it at one time and carried out an experiment with my team of six consultants, including myself. We all knew each other pretty well, but found it hard to identify which report referred to whom. Certainly the whole process told us nothing of value.

Bremner also mentions astrology. It is popular in some quarters, particularly among the young. It was recently reported that a graduate was doing the milk round and consequently had to complete a lot of application forms. Wherever she found a space at the end of the form asking her to 'Sign here', she wrote 'Capricorn'.

If you discern a note of scepticism in all this, you might just be right. But there's nowt so queer as folk. One client who asked me to recruit a finance director finished his briefing by saying, 'Finally, I don't want anyone born in 1959.' Apparently (and don't hold me to precise details) this was the year of the pig and he was a snake, and the two don't get on.

Hybrid Tests

Finally, there is a group of tests commonly used at assessment centres which I describe as 'hybrid tests' because they are neither pure tests of aptitude (in the sense that they have no right answer) or pure personality questionnaires (in that they attempt to measure various skills, often against the clock). Typical of these is the In-Tray Exercise, when a candidate is invited to sort through mountains of paper, prioritise and take appropriate action. Or a candidate might be asked to master a complex brief, to sort out the essential points from the waffle and to give a short presentation – again, with the whole exercise taking place against the clock.

There is much to be said for such a method of assessment provided the vehicle chosen is relevant. For example, if the new employee will be required to work on the telephone, it is obviously sensible to conduct part of the interviewing process by telephone. Similarly, if typing is required, a typing test is eminently sensible. In some cases a more structured approach may be appropriate. I have one client who gives all engineering candidates a design exercise, allowing about a week for preparation prior to a formal presentation followed by a question and answer session. This imaginative approach has resulted in a really high-quality engineering team.

Improving Your Performance

What should you do to improve your performance in these activities?

Clearly, if you are subjected to this as part of the 'getting to know yourself' process, play it straight. There is no point in trying to bend the rules in your favour if you seek a true bill.

As far as being assessed as a candidate is concerned, the answer is much the same, certainly with regard to personality questionnaires, which are carefully designed to spot any candidate trying to present a picture other than the truth. If someone wants to study your handwriting or draw absurd conclusions from your birth sign, there is not much you can do about it.

However, as far as aptitude tests go, you can certainly improve your scoring potential by practice. Take every opportunity to be put through such tests against the clock. Let me be quite clear – I am not suggesting that you should find out the answers and learn them; that would be cheating and anyway, because of the way the tests are constructed, pointless. But getting yourself up to speed with such tests will be beneficial and will also help you with the hybrid tests.

You can do nothing about your year of birth. If you're a pig, you're a pig.

To summarise:
* Keep an open mind about your future and consult widely.
* Consider retraining or enhancing your skills.
* Practising aptitude tests is useful.
* If you are to be exposed to psychometrics, ensure (if you can) that you are in qualified hands.
* If you are exposed to certain fashionable but questionable assessment methods, smile sweetly and acquiesce.

5

First Steps on the Job-hunting Trail

'The distance doesn't matter; it is only the first step that is difficult.'
MARQUISE DU DEFFAND

In the last chapter we discussed the options you should consider. From now on we will assume that you are looking for a full-time job.

The Clock Is Running

It is important to start your search for a job in the right way. Moving too quickly can be as unwise as moving too slowly; for example, I have already advised you against hasty networking. However, you should not 'take a break' while you sort out your ideas – this is the most dangerous concept of all.

I have met too many people who have chosen to undertake all those tasks – paint the fence, de-coke the car, paper the dining-room – which have been put on one side over recent months or years. This way lies disaster. Nor do I advise a holiday now. It will slow you down and give you the wrong attitude. Take that holiday between accepting an offer and starting work.

How often have you heard retired people say, 'I don't know how I ever found time to go to work'? Because papering the dining-room leads to thoughts about new kitchen units and painting the fence suggests that this is the time to re-lay the patio, etc. That is fine when you *have* genuinely retired, but your prime task now is to find gainful employment, and you should be busier than ever before until you reach your goal. Remember, the clock is running. Accept the fact that job-hunting is a full-time occupation.

The Rhythm of the Job-hunt

As in so many other activities, timing is a key factor in the job-hunting process. Your aim is to have, say, three or four offers in the same post so that you can choose your job. You won't succeed in meeting that aim 100%, but at least you would like to receive offers in a time-frame such that you can choose your job.

You will be surprised how long it will take to get offers. Every one of my patients has remarked repeatedly on the time taken between, for example, an advertisement appearing in the national press and any positive response. I would say that usually the gap between the appearance of the advertisement and an unconditional offer is between seven and twelve weeks (typically nine weeks).

And that is just answering advertisements. Networking is far less predictable. I can recall a patient whose first networking meeting led to a very good offer, which he accepted. But more often the first six networking letters lead to five meetings, which lead to fifteen more meetings, which lead to thirty-five more meetings. So, about four weeks after you have sent out your first set of networking letters, you are likely to have a full diary.

You must, therefore, make the best use of the early days. And there are several things you can – and indeed must – deal with fairly quickly.

What Should You Tell the World?

Your priority task is actually one of the most difficult. I am sorry to throw it at you now, but you must do it quick and you must do it right.

You must decide what you are going to tell people; apart, that is, from your spouse and your counsellor, to both of whom you told the untrammelled truth as soon as possible.

In some cases this presents no problem. For example, you work for a subsidiary company of a major conglomerate. One morning you all (all two hundred of you) arrive at work to be told that the company has been closed and everyone, without exception, employed by the company is being made redundant. Although you will probably be shocked and angry (you may even, absurdly, feel that you are somehow to blame), one thing you need not worry about is telling family, friends, colleagues (they are now ex-colleagues), recruiters, networkees and, if you feel so inclined, the tabloid press and the TV news. No secrets; no problems.

But in most cases it will be much less straightforward.

So why hurry to tell people? Because, if you don't, you will find yourself and probably your family being ostracised, and this will have a major adverse effect on your morale.

Many people have talked and written of their surprise at the treatment they received from their so-called friends when their job fell apart. I heard Freddie Laker saying on the radio that people he had known for years crossed the street to avoid him. And this anecdote is typical rather than exceptional.

In rare cases this ostracism is caused by fear. Iacocca writes that after Henry Ford had fired him he 'became somebody to be avoided at all costs ... Anyone who failed to break off complete diplomatic and social relations with me risked being fired.' I suggest that cases where ostracism is maliciously based are rare. The more usual reason people avoid someone in this position is that they are embarrassed and don't know what to say.

In many ways the death analogy applies again. If your friend's great-aunt dies at an advanced age, it is relatively easy to speak or write and give the appropriate comforting, supportive message. But in the case of a sudden and tragic death, one may be uncertain of the right thing to say or write, and consequently put off action until one's very failure to do something sooner has itself become a major embarrassment.

So it is with the loss of a job.

You will remember that chapter 1 introduced William Alexander, whose work and social life were superimposed and who suddenly lost his job – OK, he was fired. His own boss had taken the easy way out and arranged for the personnel manager to give him the sad tidings on Friday afternoon. The following morning William Alexander and his wife went shopping. They were in the local supermarket and had just started to walk, William pushing the trolley, up one of those wide aisles between banks of freezers. They saw some very good friends – another husband and wife couple, whom they had known for years and with whom they socialised a lot – turn into the far end of the same aisle, towards them, falter in their steps and then swing round so that they could avoid the meeting. William and his wife were deeply upset by this. I put it to them that it wasn't unfriendliness and disloyalty which caused their friends to cut them dead, but rather it was embarrassment. They simply didn't know what to say.

The solution – to decide what to say to them and then say it – was obvious. I am glad to say that the Alexanders' friends became extremely supportive.

What Do You Tell Your Friends and Relatives?

The first message to absorb is that you must tell the truth. Not, I hasten to add, the whole truth. After all, what is the whole truth? It might take forty-five minutes to describe and explain, and this group of people only wants to hear enough to know what supportive noises to make and what sort of help to offer. So you must keep it simple. But you must get it right first time because you are going to be networking this group and you must continue to be consistent.

However, let me emphasise: you must tell the truth. You must present the truth in the best possible way – nothing wrong with that. After all, if you were in advertising and were asked to promote a new sports car, you might emphasise its 0–60 mph performance, but you would avoid reference to its appalling fuel consumption. You are about to promote yourself in the world as the ideal candidate for a job; you want to emphasise strengths rather than weaknesses.

For me to write your script at this stage is impossible, for I don't know your precise circumstances. But we will take a couple of examples.

You work for a very large group which has recently announced 30,000 job losses (out of 250,000 employees) over the next two years. As it happens, the rest of the people with your specialisation are not going to be hit, but your new boss doesn't rate you and has suggested you should resign before you are fired. You think it over, TAKE LEGAL AND FINANCIAL ADVICE, and decide to do so, making sure that the total benefit package you negotiate is at least as good as, if not better than, the total benefit package you would have received had you genuinely been made redundant and that resignation does not affect your rights to other benefits. It is *essential* that you obtain this advice before acting thus, as resignation can affect benefits, unlike volunteering for redundancy, which shouldn't.

So, why have you left your job? Your reply might go something like this: 'Well, you've read about the group's plans for massive redundancies over the next couple of years. I could be a victim of the process, so I've resigned in order to get on with the next part of my life.'

Or, if you were in an influential senior position and had expressed views on the changes: 'You've read about the major redundancies we've planned. I didn't like the policy and opposed it strongly, so I thought it right to resign rather than to implement it.'

Or, indeed: 'I got a new boss six months ago and I'm afraid he and I just didn't get on, so I became part of that famous 80% statistic'. When asked, you cite those famous statistics which show that 80% of redundant executives had a new boss in the previous six months, and 95% in the previous two years.

Note that all these answers are short and all are the truth, packaged to protect your interests. Indeed, a brief and comforting answer of this nature will do very well until you are cross-examined closely on it.

Before being able to withstand such cross-examination you must establish your previous employer's position.

Your Previous Employer

By now it will be beginning to dawn upon you that you will in future have to answer the question 'Why have you left your job?' in much more detail at interviews and serious networking meetings. And when one of these leads to a job offer, your prospective employer (or his recruiter) will wish to speak to the boss who has been so happy to let you go. Let us call him Mr Hyde. So we now come to the whole question of your relationship with Mr Hyde.

To start with, you must decide whether or not to fight the fact that you have been fired. Obviously there is nothing to fight if you are part of a genuine 100% redundancy programme – eg a foreign group closing down its whole UK operation. But if you have been asked or invited to resign, then you must consider going to the law.

Going to the Law

I am not a lawyer and, even if I were, I would not give advice on a hypothetical case. There are many complex issues. For example, if you are an executive director of a company, there is legally a marked difference between your responsibilities and rights as an executive (an employee) on the one hand and as a director (a company officer) on the other.

Then there are the questions of wrongful and constructive dismissal – the subject of much case law.

All this is further complicated by the question of intellectual and physical property. Which leads us to the topic of restrictive clauses in your contract.

Restrictions on Future Employment

At this stage you may – depending on your circumstances – have to give some thought to any limitations on future employment as a result of restrictive clauses in your previous contract.

What I am *not* discussing here is a situation where a disgruntled employee strips quantities of data from a company's (or, indeed, a nation's) files and/or computer records, and sells them – and himself with them – to a competitor. Neither you nor I would think thus.

No, I have in mind a more typical instance where an employee has signed a perfectly reasonable confidentiality contract and is then fired. Let's say it's you. I fail to see why your previous employer can complain if you then work for a competitor – provided, I emphasise, that you do not steal information to accompany you. If your previous employer does not think you are up to the job, he should be delighted that you are henceforth going to cause havoc in the competitor's organisation and not in his.

ONCE AGAIN, I MUST EMPHASISE THAT YOU SHOULD TAKE ADVICE IF YOUR OWN PARTICULAR CIRCUMSTANCES SUGGEST MINEFIELDS AHEAD.

WIN-WIN

As a generalisation, however, I strongly believe that you should do all you can to sever relationships amicably. It is in both your interests – the classic concept of WIN-WIN negotiation. What your employer wants from you is a clean break with minimum adverse reaction within the company, no money spent on lawyers (and, possibly more important, no time spent with them), no bad publicity – in short, minimum fuss. To get all this he is likely to be co-operative, if he sees that you will be so too. Therefore, what would you like from him?

First, you need an undertaking on the reference for which he will almost certainly be asked. In the case of a written reference, it is possible to agree the actual wording. What is much more difficult is to ensure that he won't bad-mouth you on the telephone so that a conditional offer (ie an offer conditional on references and/or medical) is subsequently withdrawn. This you must avoid at all costs. So at this stage of the negotiation you need reassurance that he will give you a clean bill of health if he is telephoned about you.

What if you are sure that he is likely to say enough negative things about you to risk the offer being withdrawn? There are various ways round the problem. If the organisation is large enough, it may be possible to channel requests for references through the personnel department, who will probably provide factual information – date of joining and departure, last appointment and reason for departure (in this case resignation rather than dismissal, if you have followed the game plan so far). If you have been working for a public or institutional organisation, this shouldn't be too difficult, as such bodies tend towards the avoidance of fuss.

Alternatively, if you are suffering from the new-boss-in-the-last-six-months syndrome, you may be able to reach agreement that any reference will be dealt with by the prior boss, with whom you worked for many years and with whom you have an excellent rapport.

However, you may be coming from a small company where only one person will be involved in the reference and he or she is likely to be extremely negative about you. In that case, you will probably have to take the clear line that you left after a disagreement with your boss and that you are consequently unlikely to receive a decent reference. In which case you must cover the whole thing with other referees (a subject I discuss in detail in chapter 8). It all depends on circumstances and you must think very carefully about the implications of any plan before you decide on it.

Damning references can be damaging in both directions. From time to time law reports cover cases where the victim of a really bad reference (bad enough for a job offer to be withdrawn) has sued the originator and won. Mr Hyde or his advisers will be aware of these cases and will wish to avoid hassle if possible.

What else you require at this stage in the negotiations is very much a matter of circumstances, and all I can do is indicate a number of topics for consideration. These include retention of the company car (if you have one) for a decent period, say three or six months. To those not used to company cars (I barely knew they existed for the first twenty-seven years of my working life) this might seem like a need to cling to the trappings of office. Not so — or, rather, not altogether so. If your family life is organised on the assumption that you have your own wheels available, it is not easy to reorganise so you can cope with one less vehicle in the family. And it is not a good time to go out and buy a car. You should be aware, however, that the Inland Revenue may view the car somewhat negatively, and you should certainly take expert advice.

The car will be essential when meetings and interviews begin to crowd your diary. You also need to think about the costs of running the car and any deal you can do in this respect (even fuel, if you can manage it) will be a great help.

Next, consider asking for outplacement counselling. I have covered this topic fully in chapter 3.

You might also — and this very much depends on the exact circumstances — ask for the use of an office. Unlikely, in that it is normally sound practice to get leavers off the premises as soon as possible. But you might be able to modify this suggestion (potential for a nice touch of WIN-WIN negotiating here) and gain agreement to a degree of secretarial support — typing and, perhaps, telephone messages.

Money

These factors are, of course, all subordinate to the question of money. What terms are you offered? Have you an ally, say in the personnel department, who could massage the figures in a friendly way? Are you receiving your statutory due? Remember that most firms (over 80%) give payments above the statutory requirements.

What about your pension (very important, this, with older executives)? Do you transfer to a personal pension scheme? Take advice.

The financial complications are not over when the figures have been agreed. The way in which any monies are paid to you may have tax implications. Don't necessarily think of your previous employer as the enemy in this respect – it is in his interest to provide funds in such a way as to minimise (not of course to evade) tax liabilities.

Do nothing, sign nothing, until you have taken professional advice. If, by your positive attitude, you have won over Mr Hyde to a satisfactorily collective approach to problem solving, you will be able to get this advice free from your employer's advisers (provided you are confident of their integrity).

You would almost certainly be wise to tell your bank manager and the building society which owns your house (if applicable) at an early stage. My experience is that this is definitely a case where the No Surprises rule applies. They are both likely to be sympathetic and helpful. Your own circumstances must be the key factor, but don't make instant decisions you may regret. For example, using redundancy money to pay off your mortgage may be exactly the wrong thing to do.

My final point about money is that you should claim unemployment benefit from the DSS (Department of Social Security). Under present rules this is available for the first year regardless of how much redundancy money is involved, but this may not be so by the time you read this, so check.

Library

To get out of the house, go and check the facilities offered by your local library. In particular, does it get all the newspapers you need, not only for the appointments advertisements but also to keep an eye on items in the business and news sections that you might turn to your advantage in networking or speculative approaches?

Newspapers have another use. Most quality papers include in their weekly appointments sections articles about aspects of the employment scene and job-hunting. Read them. They are mostly instructive, up to date and stimulating. They may trigger ideas in your mind. You probably haven't bothered about them in the past, for job-hunting is rather like house-hunting. (When you have a house and have no intention of moving, you are not interested in the current state of the local housing market. When you *are* house-hunting, the housing market is top priority.) You will find that time on these articles is well spent.

Don't neglect the local press, not only for job advertisements but also for company news. Perhaps a company has announced it is to move to your area or a local company has just received a major order. Both create potential opportunities worth investigating.

Establishing friendly relations with the staff of your local library will pay dividends.

Write Your Autobiography

You must also sit down and write your autobiography. No, not a thick tome, but a few pages about yourself which will form the basis of your CV and your answers at interviews. Perhaps a couple of pages about your upbringing and education, followed by a list of your employers and jobs. List your achievements – as immodestly as you can at this stage, for this document is for the eyes of you and your counsellor, not for a potential employer.

Don't be purely descriptive. Write a couple of pages about what you particularly liked and disliked about each job. Note failures as well as successes. Try a page on interpersonal relationships at work. All this will help you to think about yourself and your work. If you carry out this task conscientiously you will be thankful that you did so during every meeting and every interview you attend.

Paperwork

This is the time to start thinking about paperwork. If you are a PC or a word-processing buff with your own equipment, you won't need outside help. Otherwise you may have to locate a secretarial agency (*Yellow Pages* or small ads in the local paper). Do not commit yourself at this stage – say, to a CV-producing company which will churn out standard rubbish. Just find out what is available, so that you know where to go when you need to.

We will look at the whole question of the administration of your job-hunt in chapter 9.

Business Cards

You may not realise it yet, but in leaving your job you have lost part
of your identity. You have been accustomed to exchanging cards with
those you meet, but now you don't have a card. And you certainly
need a card to give to somebody if you want to receive a card in
return. And you do, for the purposes of networking.

So find one of those machines scattered around in shops and
motorway service areas and produce some cards. Fifty will see you
through for a bit and they cost very little. Nothing fancy – just your
name, address and telephone number. Include your qualifications if you
like, but I would advise you to do so only if they are worth having.
There are some organisations which require only an annual cheque to
earn the initials; we all know which they are, and those initials on their
own merely point to the fact that you don't have anything more
worthwhile.

Answerphone

The other thing you need is an answerphone. Many people abhor such
things, but there are technical reasons for saying that you could miss
an interview because a recruiter could not reach you at the critical
moment. I cover the recruitment process in chapter 6, when this point
will become clear.

If, ideally, you could borrow or otherwise acquire a combined
phone/answerphone/fax system for the duration of your job-hunt, well
and good. It is this type of thing (e.g. no longer having ready access to
a fax machine) which brings home the inconvenience of losing your
job. Anything to help you find your next job must be a good thing.

Salary Aspirations

Both the last two questions in this chapter are important and difficult
to answer. First is the question: 'What salary are you seeking?' If you
have replied to an advertisement which states the salary, this question
is not all that important, in that the very fact you have replied means
you are interested in the contract as offered. The question becomes
much more difficult during networking or if you are head-hunted.

It would, obviously, be dotty for me to tell you the answer to this
question – I don't know your personal circumstances. But I will tell
you categorically how *not* to answer it: 'I don't know, I haven't really

thought about it.' That sort of reply is no way to make friends and influence people.

My personal reaction to this question when I was asked it – and I emphasise that it was my personal reaction based on my personal circumstances – was to look more at the potential than the immediate. But that was the pragmatic me. Others will tell you not to undersell yourself, and this may be good advice for you in your current personal circumstances. But whatever you do, prepare your position in advance of being asked. That position may, of course, be as much concerned with other rewards such as equity options as with straight salary.

Location

Finally, you must consider very carefully the question of location. This is a major consideration. Will you relocate? If so, are there any limitations as to where you will go? Limiting factors may be your spouse's job, children's education, aged relatives. Are you prepared to weekly commute – that is, live in digs during the week, returning home at weekends? You must face up to this issue now, lest you waste time on chasing jobs which you could not accept if offered.

In order to improve your chances, in the next chapter we will look at a recruitment operation from the enemy's camp.

To summarise:
* Accept the fact that job-hunting is a full-time activity. Don't get bogged down in domestic trivia.
* Decide what you are going to tell people.
* If possible, maintain good relations with your previous employer to get the best deal, but take professional advice before you commit yourself to anything.
* Write your autobiography.
* Get organised – business cards, answerphone, paperwork – and recce your library.
* Think carefully about the rewards you are seeking.
* Resolve the location issue.

6

Joining the Enemy

'It is right to be taught by the enemy.'

OVID

Seen from the Other End of the Telescope

Before we discuss the various methods of getting a job and plan your approach to each one, it would be helpful if you could see the recruitment process from the other side of the fence – that occupied by the employer and his advisers. So we are now going to join the enemy's ranks. I have chosen to follow through an advertised recruitment campaign as that is the most readily understood example. (This is not to say that you are most likely to find your job through an advertised appointment; as we shall see, there are other important methods to pursue.)

Let me warn you now that most recruitment consultants will say, on reading what follows, 'I don't do it like that.' Yes, of course methods vary, but the underlying principles are much the same.

A Typical Assignment

We will consider the appointment of commercial director in Shrivenham Holdings Ltd (SHL). I have chosen this title because it could mean almost anything. SHL is a medium-sized company employing 150 people. The chairman and managing director is Henry Farthington, always known as HF.

HF realises that his company is not equipped to carry out the recruitment task without help. He is too busy to do all the work himself and, in any event, is wise enough to know that he needs someone to act as a filter to ensure he does not make instant decisions based on wholly subjective grounds. There is no-one in the company who can help. HF's excellent secretary, Emma, covers the mechanistic aspects of the personnel function, but it would not be appropriate for her to carry out this assignment and to do the interviewing.

Nor would it be right to bring in the other three directors (sales, finance, production). It is not wise to let people choose a colleague who may well become a competitor for the top job later. The danger – and this is true at all levels – is that people will choose someone who lacks that inner steel to reduce the threat.

But, I hear you cry, how can you possibly advocate introducing a fifth person into the boardroom without first confirming personal chemistry? All right; there may have to be a final stage before the appointment is formally offered. In any event, the successful candidate will probably want to meet the other directors before promising to join. But in my view, HF should say to the other three directors: 'Here is X, who is going to join us as commercial director. If you don't approve, put your objection on a personal memo to me, and put your resignation in the same envelope. I will tear up one or the other of those documents.'

Of course I am exaggerating, but the underlying thought is valid and should be borne in mind by HF.

If there are a couple of non-executive directors (NEDs) things are much easier. (In companies such as this, NEDs, like spin bowlers, should always be appointed in pairs.) HF can ask them to help with this important board appointment in the final stages.

So HF decides to use a recruitment consultant to help him with the task. How does he find someone to carry out the assignment? Much the same way as one finds any professional adviser – by asking appropriate people. These might include the NEDs, the investors, the auditors, the bank manager, friends who have themselves recruited for their companies, and so on. But however HF finds his consultant, he will (after their first meeting) check him or her out by asking for and taking up references from other clients of that consultant.

The consultant who comes out of this research is David Mackintosh. I have elected myself for the job because I can tell you in detail how I would do it – as I say, methods vary, though principles remain constant.

Specification

The first stage is for me to visit HF, preferably on site at SHL so that I can get the feel of the place (in the style of Maigret), while receiving a briefing on the company, the job to be done, the person sought to fill the job and the rewards package. I will probably work from my check list to ensure that nothing is omitted, not even the hidden agenda. (Yes, there may well be a hidden agenda – see chapter 13.)

There will then be a discussion of the best method to use in order to find the right person. Initially the issue of advertisement *versus* head-hunt will be debated. We won't go into this debate here, but assume that the advertised route is selected.

Some recruiters might try the 'head-hunt backed by an advertisement' approach. In my opinion this method, which is gaining popularity, is normally a cop out. It means that a less than scrupulous consultant derives a larger fee (ie the head-hunt fee) for reading applications in response to an advertisement. There are, however, some occasions on which this approach is valid.

The meeting will conclude with my outline of how I will go about the assignment. I then go away and draft a formal proposal. The exact format varies from consultant to consultant, but always includes various essential features.

First the terms of business, including the fee and the various conditions to cover such abnormalities as failure to make an appointment or making more than one appointment from the applicants garnered from the advertisement. The fee will either be a percentage of salary (or predicted annual earnings when there is a high commission element), typically between 18% and 25% for an advertised assignment. That sounds simple enough, but some consultants quote for a percentage of total benefits rather than basic salary and evaluate such benefits as a car or health insurance in arriving at the figure from which to calculate a percentage (I do not approve of such an approach). So HF needs to be very sure what the rules are before he accepts. The proposal also includes the suggested, and costed, advertising plan.

Secondly, the proposal includes a job description which describes the company, the job to be done and the rewards.

Thirdly, the specification of the person sought. I call this the 'employee specification', but other descriptions are regularly used such as 'person specification' and 'candidate profile'. Sometimes this document and the job description are packaged in one document, frequently called the 'job specification'. These titles are not critical, but the contents are essential.

The Choice of Advertisement

Finally, the draft advertisement. The plan, which was discussed in detail at the meeting, will be based on an open or blind advertisement.

By this I mean that an open advertisement discloses the name of the client company (SHL in this case), whereas a blind advertisement conceals it.

The decision whether to go open or blind depends on several interrelated factors. It is highly desirable to put the job's location in the advertisement. Location is one of the critical factors a potential candidate considers before deciding whether or not to apply. You will recall that I said (in chapter 5) it was essential for you, as a job-hunter, to decide at an early stage what, if any, are your geographical limitations. Many people scanning the pages of job advertisements look at the location first.

It is also highly desirable to put the salary in an advertisement – salary is another parameter by which potential candidates scan advertisements. I have attended seminars when analysts in the recruitment field have said that omitting salary from an advertisement will reduce the response by a factor as high as seven. That is probably pushing it, but I have no doubt an advertisement without a salary is far less effective than one with it.

Furthermore, potential candidates have a strong preference for knowing the company to which they are applying. Typically, omission of the name of the company may reduce the response by a third. The rule I apply is that, if someone makes an application in response to a blind advertisement, I do not disclose the name of the applicant to my client until I have cleared it with the applicant. However, it is very understandable that a job-seeker might be nervous about applying for a job in an unknown company, in case he is applying for his own job, and you, as a job-hunter, cannot be sure that the consultant with whom you are dealing has the necessary integrity. This is why the response is always lower in the case of a blind advertisement.

Now comes the rub. In many cases the client wishes to conceal from the other employees the salary which will be paid to the new senior executive. However, if the advertisement is blind (in that it conceals the company's name) but discloses the location, together with a helpful description of the company and the job, it will in most cases be relatively easy for the employees to guess that it is their company. So a blind advertisement which discloses location and salary will conceal the identity of the company from the potential candidates, who may be put off from applying, while not concealing it from employees (and, perhaps, competitors), which was the purpose of making the advertisement blind.

(By now you are tuned in to the philosophy of job-hunting. You will enthusiastically reply to blind advertisements or those which which omit salary; box numbers, even. Because in these cases your chances of an interview are improved.)

Response to the Advertisement

Well, all this has been thrashed out and the written proposal puts it all together. HF accepts, and the advertisement duly appears in the appropriate newspaper or magazine. It asks for a written response.

What happens next depends to some extent on the type of job and the medium in which the advertisement has been placed. Some years ago Professor C. Northcote Parkinson wrote (in, I think, *Parkinson's Law*) that the perfect advertisement produces one applicant who matches the specification exactly. Sadly, the process is not that perfect.

If the job is very specialised and is advertised in a specialist medium, the response will probably be numerically small (say up to fifty) and I will read each letter and attached CV with great care as it arrives, making arrangements to interview suitable applicants as soon as possible. The whole process, from your point of view as a job-hunter, is reasonably precise. If the advertisement seeks, for example, an expert in cobalt mining who speaks fluent Russian and Mandarin, and you are that rare animal, your application will be welcomed with relief and you can expect an early phone call.

That situation is rare. Much more likely is a generally phrased advertisement with a specification which opens the door to a large number of applications. These days it is not uncommon to receive six hundred applications in response to an advertisement placed in one of the major broadsheets, and I heard of one recently which produced over three thousand applications.

So I watch and wait. If the advertisement appears on, say, a Thursday, roughly half the response will have flooded into the office by the following Tuesday (if a Sunday paper, by the Wednesday). And if by this time I have, say, three hundred applications, I can leave it to my staff to collect and collate, and make a note in my diary to screen all the applications in about a week's time, ie ten to twelve days after the advertisement appeared.

Screening

You must imagine me, a week later, sitting at my desk or table in my office or house with a pile of five hundred and fifty applications in front of me. (The last fifty, from people overseas or on holiday, will drift in over the next fortnight.) From these I must select between fifteen and thirty candidates to interview.

In some consultancies this screening process is delegated – perhaps to a trainee consultant or to a senior secretary. In my opinion this is bad practice, for only by going through this mountain of bumf can I get a feel for the market.

In later chapters we will discuss CVs and letters, and I will make didactic remarks about what is or is not acceptable. While you are disagreeing and, for example, producing a six-page CV, just think of me looking at that paper mountain.

How long do you think I spend on each application? I often ask new patients to guess how long a recruiter will spend on a CV, and their answers range from three to ten minutes, typically five minutes. Well, five minutes repeated three hundred and fifty times is twenty-nine hours and ten minutes. Allowing for breaks every now and again to drink a cup of coffee or bang one's head against a wall, this would be a full 40-hour week. And, I can assure you, I will not spend a week on this screening process.

Try thirty seconds per application.

Obviously it would be very bad professional practice for a recruitment consultant, engaged in a critical task from the client's viewpoint, to make three hundred and fifty major decisions each in thirty seconds, so most of us use a staged process. In some organisations the delegated screener referred to above may extract the obviously unsuitable candidates. I don't like the idea, because this will probably be done using easily measurable parameters – 'reject anyone over forty-seven, Bill' or 'I don't want to see the papers of anyone without a degree, Sally' – and anyone who has something unusual but special to offer will be missed.

Personally, I go through the pile fast, putting each application on to either the 'look at again' pile or the 'reject' pile. At the same time I use a 5-level grading system to aid subsequent dithering. If in doubt I use the 'look at again' pile, and would hope to have forty to fifty in that pile at the end of the first run. But that run is quick – you can't get away from the fact – so the aim of the application (i.e. letter and CV together) is *look at me in detail, please*. And you only have thirty seconds to achieve that.

Having divided the applications into two piles, I go through the 'look at again' pile in more detail. Obviously the sensitivity of the next filter depends on how many there are in this pile. If, for example, there are sixteen, I would arrange to see them all. But it is more likely that the pile contains many more applications than the number of interviews I wish to undertake.

There are fifty-two in this case. I will now put these into three groups. First, those whom I definitely want to interview – let's say eleven. Thirdly, those who now join the 'reject' pile after a closer look – let's say twenty-three – and secondly, in the middle, (in this case eighteen of them) applications about which I want more information before deciding whether or not to invest 1½ hours of my time plus travelling expenses (at my client's cost).

I plan to interview a maximum of twenty-four candidates, so I don't want more than thirteen of these eighteen.

Telephone Interviews

Now we embark on the telephone interviews – which, if properly done, do not appear to be interviews at all. Quite a lot of recruiters do this, or so it seems from the feedback I receive from my outplacement patients, who often tell me about telephone calls they receive which at first sight appear to be routine.

What I do is to note a couple of questions on each letter of application, and then sort the eighteen applications into order of priority. Then Pat Berry goes to work. The reason she does the telephone interviews is that it's difficult for me to ask a couple of questions and not follow them up with an offer of an interview. But Pat can say, after the appropriate introduction and greetings, something like this:

> 'Mr Mackintosh has read your application with interest. He is currently drawing up his interview list and has asked me to get some supplementary information before he finalises it. We note that you have quintuplets in the middle of their A Levels. What are your plans for relocating to the new job should you get it – and if you plan to weekly commute would you look to your new employer to provide your accommodation?'

The answer is of interest, but of equal interest is the impression the applicant gives on the phone. At the end of the discussion Pat can thank him and say that we will be in touch shortly, without the need to make a firm commitment.

Language Interviews by Telephone

If the advertisement calls for advanced language skills (eg 'fluent in English and two other European languages') I try to avoid futile and time-wasting interviews by arranging preliminary telephone interviews in the language or languages claimed by those candidates who appear to fit the specification otherwise.

To this end I have a team of home-working linguists, whom I call upon when the need arises. Thus a candidate who claims to be fluent in, say, Polish may answer the telephone one evening and hear nothing but Polish from the caller. I have learnt that candidates who genuinely are fluent or near fluent not only pass this test but also enjoy it, appreciating this professional approach to the screening process.

Being Available

You will now see why I lay such stress on installing an answerphone at home. When Pat sits down with eighteen applications in order of priority, she has to pass on to the next one if there is no reply to her phone call. If, on the other hand, you have an answerphone, she can at least leave a message and the risk of your missing an interview is diminished.

If you have a day-time phone number where you can be reached, it should be included — preferably in the CV (for that is where we look for phone numbers), but, if not there, in the letter. Although you are jobless, you may have some locum work or you may go every day to an outplacement firm's offices or to an executive job club — that number should be included. And make it clear that it is acceptable for the recruitment team to call you there; we are very nervous, for reasons of confidentiality, about calling applicants at work unless they specifically say we may.

You will understand by now that the whole screening process, i.e. from initial application to the first interview, is the chanciest part of the whole process for the candidates.

The Lobby and Known Faces

While all this is going on, two additional categories of candidates will emerge.

First, there is the group whom I refer to as the Lobby. This comprises people who believe that there is an advantage to be gained by cutting out the middle man and going direct to HF. There isn't, because HF would not spend vast sums on my fee if he wanted to wade through piles of paper himself. Just before the advertisement appeared I wrote to HF, saying that he would inevitably receive some letters of this nature. My advice to him was that he should pass the applications to me and I would deal with them in the normal way.

The more interesting second group consists of known faces. In some cases candidates who know HF will write to him direct, a sort of lobby with knobs on. I suggested to HF that he should send them a short letter, thanking them for their interest and saying that he was passing applications to me. On my copy of each letter he should make a note as to whether or not he was interested in that candidate.

Other candidates will write to me saying that they know HF. In these cases I check that the candidates are happy to have their interest revealed to HF (confidentiality is essential in the recruitment business and one should never assume anything about disclosing names) and then I ask HF about them. Sometimes HF will say 'Oh, good, I hoped that Harriet Jones would apply. I couldn't approach her direct because doing so would have caused difficulties in the Chamber of Commerce, but now she's applied we should look at her very carefully – could be dead right for the job.'

At other times HF will say 'Oh dear, I was afraid that Roger Wetherby might apply. He's wrong for the job, but as he's the buying manager of my main customer, I don't want to harm the relationship by rejecting him outright.' I then have to conduct one of the most difficult types of interview, namely one in which my sole aim is to get Wetherby to withdraw (perhaps because I undersell the job to him) so that the HF/Wetherby relationship may continue without aggro.

Let us return to SHL (Shrivenham Holdings Ltd). I now have my programme and I see twenty-four candidates in an appropriate interview room (not on the client's site at this stage).

Late Applications

While these interviews are under way, the final applications will filter in from people who were on holiday or on business overseas. It is sometimes suggested by outplacement consultancies that there is some advantage in being a late applicant, on the theory that the consultant will give it more attention. This is nonsense. If the response is large and the initial interview list looks good, I will put the late applicants on hold just to cover my position in case the initial interviews prove disappointing. If, on the other hand, the response is small, I will have moved very quickly to interview suitable looking candidates; a late entry will have been overtaken by events. The idea that you gain in some way by applying three weeks after the advertisement has appeared is wrong.

The Recruiter's Aim

We will discuss the interview process in a later chapter. At this stage I will merely say that during each interview I am asking myself one main question: 'Should I put this candidate on the short-list?' To get there I have to ask three supplementary questions:

a. 'Has this candidate got the knowledge, experience and personality to do the job?'
b. 'How well will he or she get on with HF?'

> This is the *Blind Date* aspect of my work, and is the most testing. This is the time when I must suppress my own personal chemistry and try to see the candidate through HF's eyes. I cannot overemphasise the importance of this aspect. Take two candidates, X and Y, who have similar skills and experience. The difference is that X likes to agree his budget and to be left to get on with the job, while Y prefers continuous communication with his boss and colleagues to ensure that the whole team is working together. One style is not better than the other: they are simply different. If I wish to choose either X or Y for the short-list, the decision as to who gets the spot depends on HF's style of managing his company. If you, a candidate, are turned down after interview for an appointment for which you seem exceptionally suited, it will probably be for reasons of a perceived mismatch of your style with that of the future employer, and you should not take it as a personal slight.

c. 'Is this a genuine candidate from the logistics viewpoint?'

> By logistics I mean the implications of rewards, location and availability. If, for reasons of relativity, HF's absolute top negotiating position for salary is £37.5K (let's say the job was advertised at c. £35K), then it is pointless to short-list a candidate who will not, in any circumstance, make the move for less than £40K. It may be possible to shift this position by discussion of the whole benefits package (including, perhaps, equity participation), but if those are the ultimate negotiating positions, then best call it a day.
>
> Equally, it is necessary to clear the location issue at a early stage. I have already discussed the principal restrictions on mobility – spouse's job, children's education, housing – and nothing is worse than to have a successful candidate drop out shortly before joining because of late family pressure against the move.

Availability is usually less of a problem, but should be explored. For example, it is not uncommon for a candidate to say 'Well, I couldn't join until the beginning of August [it is now January] because I can then exercise my share options. Unless, of course, HF is willing to recompense me to the tune of £25,000 for the loss of those options.'

I must discuss these points at this stage so that I can present HF with a clear statement on rewards, relocation (if necessary) and availability for everyone on the short-list.

The final act of the first interview is for me to give the candidate a clear statement of what will happen next and by when, concluding with, 'Don't call us, we'll call you.' This saves unnecessary office time responding to candidates asking for an update. It goes without saying that one must stick to the plan and give an answer by the promised date.

Throughout the assignment I have been discussing progress with HF. Employers often view recruitment consultants as necessary but expensive evils, and it does no harm to keep reminding my client what a busy bee I am. Now is the time to present HF with a short-list.

The Short-list

On occasions it may be right to discuss the possible runners with the client before going firm on the short-list, but I would much rather not. In this case my relationship with HF is excellent and he is, after all, paying me quite a lot of money to find him a short-list of suitable candidates. I have met the candidates and he hasn't, so I must make the decision as to whom I should include.

The size of the short-list is a function of:

a. The quality of the field (and by quality I mean suitability *vis-à-vis* the specification rather than underlying virtue; the purpose of recruitment is to find the most suitable person rather than the best).
b. The number of subsequent stages in the process.

In this case I tell HF that I want him to meet five candidates, with the provisional plan to take those with whom he is happiest (probably two) to a final selection panel involving, in addition to HF, the two non-executive directors. If it subsequently turns out, from the short-list interviews, that there is one candidate with whom HF is totally enamoured, we would then modify the plan and bring in the non-executive directors more in the rubber stamp mode than the selection mode.

Short-lists are an organisational nightmare. For the first short-list I have got to get seven people (HF, five candidates and myself) in one location on the same day to a programme, and for the short short-list about six (HF, two NEDs, two candidates and myself). The lesson for you as a job-hunter is always to make yourself available — at least that may give you some small advantage over the busy executive who cannot be present on the chosen day.

The format of the short-list interviews will depend on HF's views, preferably as advised by me. Personally I like to sit in, so that I can get it right in the next round if the day turns out to be a disaster. But some clients feel inhibited (and there is, in any event, a lot to be said for one-to-one communication), in which case I slip away (having forewarned the candidates) after the introduction and the ceremonial pouring of the coffee, returning after an agreed interval.

Second Meetings

Returning to the First Principle of War, it is essential that HF has his aim right. The question he has to answer is not 'Do I want this candidate as my commercial director?' but rather, 'Do I wish to see this candidate again?' Only a fool would make such an important appointment after one meeting (and a somewhat artificial meeting at that). Second meetings are critical. Sometimes I short-list a candidate with whom I have spent an hour and a half at first interview, and cringe inwardly at short-list — our second meeting — while I wonder why I made such a stupid selection. In much the same way, HF will need to see his new commercial director twice more before offering the job, once with his non-executive directors and once informally — over dinner or whatever.

We then go through the final stages of negotiating the fine detail of the package. This negotiation must be done by HF and the successful candidate — the recruiter merely acts as a lubricant or, in the modern jargon, a facilitator. Then a conditional offer, subject to references and possibly a medical inspection, is made. I discuss the whole question of referees elsewhere. The offer is then made unconditional provided the references stack up.

Unsuccessful Candidates

Thus far I have tracked the successful candidate. Naturally it is important to handle sympathetically those who have fallen by the wayside. For reasons of time and cost most rejections must be done by letter, but I always telephone bad news to those whom I have short-listed and who have been filtered out. The most painful part of the job is telling the unsuccessful candidate of the last two. To be so close to that glittering prize and not to grasp it is distressing.

Occasionally I have a particularly difficult situation. Let us say that HF would like to employ candidate A, but would be happy to consider candidate B if A drops out. Now we start to play games. My job, on behalf of HF, is to keep B happy whilst we work on A. Meanwhile A may be trying to up the ante. My negotiating position (technically I am not negotiating, but it may help to give the impression that I am) depends on how ready HF is to take B if A drops out. Recruitment frequently becomes really difficult after the short-list.

So what's this to you, as a candidate? It will become very important when you have one offer and are waiting for another. If you refuse the first, do you finish up with nothing? We will discuss all this in the chapter concerned with handling offers.

You now have an insight into the advertised recruitment process from the other side of the desk — or rather, in these days of user-friendly interviews, across the knee-high coffee table. But replying to advertise-ments is only one way of finding a job. Let's look at them all in the next chapter.

To summarise
* The chanciest part of replying to an advertisement is getting through the first screening.
* Don't be put off by blind advertisements, advertisements without salaries or advertisements with box numbers. Your chances of an interview are improved and you don't have to accept the job if it is of-fered.
* Your application has thirty seconds to make an impression.
* Be accessible — answerphone and day-time telephone number.
* Emphasise your immediate availability to start work.

7

Who's Who in the Job Scene

'Knowledge itself is power.'
FRANCIS BACON

The Six Ways to Get a Job

How do you get a job? There are, I suggest, six possible ways:

1. Through an advertisement.
2. By approaching or registering with the recruitment industry, which in itself can be divided into three categories:
   a. Head-hunters (search)
   b. Advertised recruitment consultants (selection)
   c. Body-shops (agencies)
   although these interact to some extent.
3. Direct approaches to potential employers.
4. Networking.
5. Tapping the hidden job market.
6. Luck.

In this chapter we are going to look at these methods and the players in the game.

Through an Advertisement

I put this first because it is the one with which we are all most familiar — or think we are. Whether or not it will necessarily be the most fruitful method of finding a job (and it probably won't be) depends on a variety of factors (eg age, qualifications, experience), but it is a method you cannot ignore.

There are divided views about responding to advertisements: some outplacement firms teach that you should reply only to advertisements when you match the advertised specification to a high degree, say 70%, and not at all if there is some GO/NOGO criterion you cannot match, such as an accountancy qualification.

I don't entirely agree, because I know of too many cases where an application in response to a non-matching advertisement has led to a job. Indeed, this happened to me when I left the Army at the age of forty-five. I answered an advertisement for consultants aged between twenty-eight and thirty-five. Fortunately for me, the two decision-makers in the company (ICFC Consultants – later 3i Consultants) were Gerry Richardson and Rodney Drew. They looked past the age factor (which an unimaginative and mechanistic recruiter would have treated as a NOGO) and invited me to join the company. I could quote more examples in this vein.

In the last chapter we observed an advertised recruitment assignment through the wrong end of the telescope. In due course, once you have got yourself organised and written your CV, we will look at advertisements – where they appear, what they say and how to reply to them. Let us leave advertisements there for the present.

The Recruitment Industry

I divide the recruitment industry into three groups. There is a certain snobbery in the recruitment world and the *élite* are normally considered to be the big executive search firms or head-hunters. So you will frequently hear anyone in the recruitment world refer to himself or herself as a head-hunter – even, perhaps, someone filing CVs in a body-shop. This is a pity, as a good body-shop is just as valuable to a manager as a good search company, if not more so.

Head-hunters

In principle, head-hunters exist because the right person for a particular job may be happily employed and not looking for a move, and thus not reading the appointments columns. It is, therefore, the head-hunter's task to identify likely candidates, track them down, grill them without being too blatant about it (in head-hunting the rubber truncheon is wrapped in cottonwool) and generally seduce them. So there are no applicants in a head-hunt, only candidates.

Let's take a simple (facile, indeed) example. Borchester General Hospital needs a new boss for its brain surgery unit. It has a total of twenty-four staff (surgeons, doctors, nurses, technicians). For a number of reasons the appointment cannot be filled internally.

The likely candidates are the bosses of smaller units who want to increase the scope of their responsibilities and the second-in-commands or bright up-and-comers in larger units who want to run their own shows. So the head-hunter, who will go through the same briefing and specification process as for the advertised recruitment I described in the previous chapter, will ask the research department to dig out the names of all the people who fall into these categories, plus any other possible people they can think of – say a distinguished brain surgeon who has taken a couple of years off to do research in a rich American university. The research department will also list people who are on the fringe of the business including, perhaps, retired brain surgeons with good contacts.

Technically all these people are 'sources' rather than 'candidates' – i.e. sources of information. Now somebody (either the researcher or the head-hunter – different organisations do it differently) telephones all these sources and describes the appointment (usually under the cloak of confidentiality at this stage), and then asks if the source can suggest anyone who might be suitable and interested. If the source is really a potential candidate, the questioning may become more direct. After a great many phone calls – hundreds perhaps – a list of suitable candidates, who both meet the specification and who are interested, is produced. These candidates are then interviewed.

There are obvious advantages in this system. For example, it is much easier to retain confidentiality by these surreptitious phone calls than it is by sticking an advertisement four columns wide and 12 cm deep in one of the quality national daily or Sunday newspapers. But there is also a potential conflict of interest, which can make life difficult for head-hunters.

The dilemma is this. Consider Ruth Williamson, a head-hunter working for Smith, Jones & Robinson, the internationally-famed search consultancy. She is recognised as the leading head-hunting expert on whisky distillers and, when a top distillery company needs a new technical director, the managing director approaches her to undertake the task.

But Williamson became the expert by head-hunting in the industry and establishing a record of successful appointments. Many of the top distillers have been her clients. One of the rules of the game is that a head-hunter does not (or certainly should not) go back and seduce key players in companies about which she (in this case) has privileged information – at least, not for a specified period of time. So that is the dilemma: the more expert a head-hunter is in a specific industry sector, the more restricted may be the field in which to search.

From the employer's viewpoint head-hunting has the advantage of confidentiality and the ability to find candidates who are not actively job-hunting, but the disadvantage is that the successful candidate has to be tempted into making the move, and it is more difficult to keep within salary (or total rewards) limits.

From what I have said you, the job-hunter, may feel that head-hunters aren't going to be much interested in you, since the thrust of a search is directed at people already in jobs. And in the booming mid-1980s there was, I think, an element of truth in the concept that people out of jobs were not readily welcomed by head-hunters. Not so today. First, because there are lots of good people on the market – you're one of them. Secondly, because in grim employment times (possibly the early 1990s, possibly the whole of the 1990s, possibly forever?) people in jobs are much less inclined to make a move, with all the potential risks of things going wrong. So head-hunters are willing, indeed anxious, to look at those without jobs as well as those with. Indeed, in the most recent (as I draft this) search I have observed from the employer's side of the table as his adviser, the head-hunter of one of the best known search firms produced a short-list of three, all of whom were unemployed. (None of them met the specification, but not for that reason.)

So you must get your CV on the files of the search firms. Not easy, however, as their daily post-bags bulge with CVs, not all of which are actually read or even retained. Much the best way is to get at the head-hunter through more devious means, not least networking.

I discuss networking in detail later in the book, but, while we are talking about head-hunters, let me describe one example. Henry Blake, who was a patient of mine, networked, *inter alia*, Hermione Carstairs. They had worked in the same company some years earlier. She had by now reached the appointment of human resources director of a major international plc. At the networking meeting Carstairs gave Blake the name of a head-hunter she used for certain senior appointments. When the head-hunter received Blake's networking letter he agreed to meet him. Naturally he was not going to reject someone introduced by one of his key clients, so Blake was assured of at least a meeting with that head-hunter and it was then up to him to get himself put on the register.

The message is, therefore; get on to the files of as many search companies as you can. Who are these search companies?

First there are the 'pure' search firms. You can identify them from various reference books in the library and from talking to experienced business friends. You will not see their advertisements in the press because they are pure searchers, although many of them have now set up sister firms which do advertised recruitment. A spokesman for one of the major search firms was reported in the press as saying: 'We have set out to capture business which was being reluctantly passed to the recruitment advertising specialists. We were not sure that they did a good job for our clients.' I hope for his own sake that he was incorrectly quoted – or alternatively that he can afford some larger hats.

Then there are substantial firms which do both advertised recruitment and search. Again, the reference books will identify them for you. As I mentioned in chapter 6, there are those who do both simultaneously – an approach about which I have certain reservations.

Finally, there are the small firms and independents which either do search alone or both search and selection. As ever, my view of these is that the good ones are excellent (but then I'm prejudiced, because Mackintosh Enterprises falls into this category) and the bad ones rubbish. In your role as a job-hunter that is not important – your aim is to get yourself known as being available, by as many people as possible. Don't worry if a job you are head-hunted for is not good enough or if the consultant doing the job is an obvious nincompoop. If you follow the trail, you may discover a better job in the background. Always remember that you can never turn down a job until you have been offered it.

Advertised Recruitment Consultants

I have already described the advertised recruitment process; it is sometimes referred to as 'selection'. Obviously it is easy to find out what firms these are – look in the papers, magazines and journals.

Some firms cover all types of appointment – clearly the big firms, who annually produce acres of advertisements, do so. There are also firms which specialise in certain industries, skills, employment styles (eg overseas contract appointments) and locations. If such firms are of interest to you, how do you identify them? After all, there are around 1,000 selection firms in the country – you can't approach them all.

It's obvious, really. If, for example, you seek a job in telecommunications, you look at the job advertisements in all the specialist telecommunication magazines, working through a few back copies if possible. (Your library, a professional or trade body, or a firm in the industry with a good library should be able to help here.) List each recruitment consultancy which has advertised jobs, and give one tick for each advertisement. You will soon identify the companies which advertise regularly for the telecommunications industry. Those are the ones to approach.

Or perhaps your specialisation is patio engineering. Acquire copies of the various journals, magazines and/or newspapers of IPE (the Institute of Patio Engineering) and go through the same exercise.

Locality is more difficult, as many jobs are never advertised in the local press. So you turn to *Yellow Pages* – at least you will see who claims to be a recruitment consultant in your area.

Getting yourself on to the registers of selection consultancies is difficult in that many of them don't keep registers. If any given consultancy receives an average of six hundred replies to an advertisement of general appeal, it means that there is hardly a shortage of candidates. So on receiving a new assignment, it is easier to stick a new advertisement in the paper than to wade through three thousand applications from the last five similar assignments. Thus I advise you not to become one of those job-hunters who spend vast amounts of time and money mail-shotting hundreds of consultancies. Do it selectively, networking wherever possible.

In the 1980s a lot of selection consultancies put every candidate into some form of blood-bank; not many do so these days. One of the reasons why blood-banks can be a waste of time and money is that people who get jobs do not always bother to write to the large number of contacts, head-hunters, recruitment consultants, companies, etc. with whom they have been in touch during their job searches. Blood-banks are, therefore, normally out of date.

There is a moral in this – a really important action that meets two of your requirements simultaneously. If you are on any files, registers, databases or whatever, you should remind the holders of those storage systems of your presence from time to time. Not too often, or you'll be identified as a nuisance and a fuss-budget. However, what you can do is to write occasionally to those individuals and organisations who appear to be genuinely interested in you with, for example, a new CV – perhaps including some temporary or consultancy work you have been doing or, to take another example, to tell them that you have just taken a three-month contract overseas and giving your new availability date.

Provided you avoid the aforementioned fuss-budget style, the consultant will be grateful for this, because it will be clear that you will extract yourself from the blood-bank when you eventually do find a job, and this is particularly important with people you've met, e.g. someone who short-listed you for a job you didn't get. Your helpful attitude may cause your file to be activated to your advantage if, for example, an employer says to the consultant: 'I need a new production manager, but don't want to spend £5,000 on an advertisement. Have you got anyone suitable on your books?'

This worked for a patient called Andrew Pritchley. He had been short-listed for a job, which he didn't get, by a consultant working for a large selection firm. Pritchley got a locum job for six months and told the consultant, who obviously appreciated this and put Pritchley into the company's system. Four months later Pritchley was invited for an interview by another consultant in the same firm, but in a different office two hundred miles away.

Body-shops

All of which leads us conveniently to employment agencies or recruitment agencies, often referred to as body-shops.

The simplest example is an agency dealing in temporary staff. A secretary is going on holiday. The firm is too small to cover the job, so someone phones the agency to get a temporary secretary for a fortnight.

There are also body-shops for permanent jobs. Indeed, in the Pritchley example I gave above, the selection firm was being used as a body-shop: 'Have you got a suitable body on your shelves that you can sell me for an appropriate fee?'

You probably think of body-shops as being restricted to temporary and low-paid jobs. Not necessarily so. There are specialist agencies who deal with jobs at all levels. Indeed, going back to the example of the brain surgeon for Borchester General Hospital, it may be that a body-shop specialising in brain surgeons is able to come up with the right person.

Whether or not you should get yourself on to the books of one or more body-shops is a matter of your age, experience, specialisation. For example, if you are a university student looking for vacation work, it is something – but not the only thing – you could do. Interesting and useful vacation work is a very good thing for you to have on your CV when you graduate.

Licences

The organisations I have described have to hold a licence, issued by the Employment Agency Licensing Office, which is part of the Department of Employment. The number of this licence should be on the company's (or individual's) writing-paper. If you are in any way concerned that an advertisement has been used to trawl the market for some nefarious purpose such as increasing a junk mailing list, please get in touch with the Department of Employment, either to say that some licensee is breaking the rules or to say that someone is operating illegally (i.e. without a licence).

Fees

Finally, in the professional scene, a word about fees. In the case of permanent appointments the recruiter's fee is paid by the employer. As a candidate you should pay nothing to a recruiter. This is not universally the case. When interviewing in Singapore, I was fascinated to learn that it is fairly common – normal, indeed – for recruiters to play both ends against the middle and take a fee from the employer and another from each candidate.

In the case of temporary appointments, it is normal for the employer to pay the agency, and the agency to pass on the temp's pay less a cut.

Direct Approaches to Potential Employers

Of all the methods of looking for a job, that of approaching potential employers direct is the one about which I find it most difficult to be didactic.

Let's be clear – I'm talking here about speculative, out-of-the-blue approaches. Of course you are going to approach potential employers in a number of ways – job advertisements placed by the companies themselves, indirectly through advertisements placed by selection consultants, indirectly through head-hunters and, above all, through your network. But is it worth writing speculative letters direct to potential employers?

There is one type of approach we can discard immediately (although some books and outplacement consultants still, fatuously, recommend it). This is when a job-hunter writes to the boss of some company, perhaps two hundred miles away, saying – and I abbreviate, because it is too painful to go into detail: 'I am looking for a job ... here's my CV ... I am going to be in your area on Thursday ... I would like to get your advice about employment in your area ... I will look in at 11 am and hope that you will have time to give me your advice.'

Why is this fatuous? First, because it is barefaced cheek to ask a total stranger for advice (and consequently time). Secondly, because it is a blatant con trick. Lastly, it is a waste of a good opportunity. If the company concerned really is a good prospect, then it should be networked properly. Once you have made a mess of approaching a company, it is very hard to do it properly a second time.

Leaving that sort of rubbish aside, let's consider the two main opinions. The first school of thought says that the trick is to get at the decision-maker before he sends for his personnel director or recruitment consultant and initiates a planned recruitment. Anecdotal evidence suggests that a speculative letter may catch the chairman or managing director at just the right moment. I can recall a client who proudly told me that he could save the outrageous cost of advertising and my even more outrageous fee by appointing someone whose letter happened to arrive in his in-tray the very morning of our briefing meeting. (I saw this character and very good he was too; he was appointed and did a super job.)

Some years ago I heard the chairman of a substantial plc say that he read every speculative letter addressed to him and had made some useful appointments therefrom, though in this case it was not clear if these letters were, in fact, networking letters with a key name in the introduction or purely speculative – some of them must have been the latter from the point he was making. I even read of a chief executive who, as a result of a speculative letter, embarked on a reorganisation he had been thinking about for some time and appointed the speculator to an appropriate job.

And yet, I wonder. I have talked to many chairmen and chief executives who have said that they are fed up with the piles of junk mail – including letters from speculative job-hunters – which arrive at their offices. In many cases their secretaries bin such letters – unless, of course, there is a key name which demands that it should be passed to the boss. As I've said, my concern is that a speculative approach of this type, which merely causes irritation, may muddy the waters subsequently when a perfectly acceptable networked approach becomes available. But there may be cases where the speculative, out-of-the-blue approach is right. In which case, it is essential that you do your homework, not only on the *raison d'être* (which you may have gleaned from the business pages of the heavy press, for example) but also on the detail. There is, for example, no more certain way to ensure that your letter dies a rapid death than to spell the recipient's name incorrectly.

When the homework is done properly it can, however, pay dividends. In an article in the *Daily Telegraph* about the milk-round for graduates, Brian Steptoe, Director of the University of London Careers Advisory Service, was reported as telling a highly relevant story about focused research: 'I was in Exeter the other day and I spoke to one student who had seen an article in his local paper saying that an insurance company was opening an office in the city. He dashed off an application to the personnel manager in London and got a job there within six weeks.'

Exhibitions

One potentially useful source of information about a company is its exhibition stand. If you are seeking work in a specific market sector, e.g. health care, hotels or telecommunications, a visit to that industry's exhibition or trade fair should give you bags of information about products and future developments.

Don't disclose the reason for your interest, since you may be after the job of the person who is providing all this information.

You will find details of relevant exhibitions in the appropriate specialist/trade magazines. There is, also, a booklet called *Exhibition Bulletin*, published monthly by the London Bureau (details at appendix 1). Your friendly library will probably get you a copy if you ask the staff nicely.

Networking

By now you will have realised that networking is my nap selection for these methods. You mustn't start too early, lest you send the wrong message. And you must write your CV beforehand – which we haven't done yet. So wait until we get to chapter 12.

Tapping the Hidden Job Market

There is much talk in the outplacement world of hidden vacancies, although I am not quite sure what this means. Provided you are networking busily (which means using personal contacts effectively), establishing good relationships with professional recruiters and approaching suitable companies (but only when you can't network them), there doesn't seem to be a lot left. But keep thinking – there is always another angle. Early in 1993 it was reported that someone put seven hundred and fifty copies of his CV under the windscreens of likely-looking executive cars. He found a job, although the reports did not make it clear if it resulted from one of those seven hundred and fifty CVs. Whether or not that was the case, we can definitely say that he was an energetic job-hunter – which put him ahead of the field.

Luck

I can't help you here. There is a well-known saying: 'You make your own luck.' Rubbish. What you can do is exploit it. So if the chap next to you in the public bar tells the landlord he is looking for a new sales director, and you fit the bill, jump in. Buy him a pint and let him beat you at darts or pool. Who knows, it might be just the way you get that elusive job.

To summarise:
* Do not neglect any of the methods of job-hunting. They are all valid.
* Keep your contacts in the picture, but in a low-key, unfussy way.
* If you have to make speculative approaches, do your homework. But it's better to network.
* Don't neglect exhibitions as a source for your research.
* Be imaginative, ever ready to exploit an opportunity.

8

Don't Send Him Off, Ref

'There was a saying, much quoted in the war years, that if an Englishman told you he was a secret agent it was a lie, and that if an American told you the same thing, it was true.'

NOËL COWARD

Why Referees?

From time to time there is an outburst of stories in the press about people who have gained appointments by false pretences. Headlines such as 'How I Became a Bogus Doctor' and 'Bogus Guy's Manager Is Sent to Jail' abound. Not all the stories are medical; some concern good old-fashioned crime, as for example when an ex-lag got a job as a warehouseman in a high security warehouse at Heathrow, using phoney references, in order to get his hands on cash and jewellery.

Employers just don't learn. Take the case referred to above, in which a biology teacher, who had spent two years in prison for posing as a doctor, got a job as a manager at Guy's Hospital. Subsequently a spokesman for the hospital said that in future non-medical staff 'must show documentary evidence of qualifications'. Is it really a secret that documents can be forged?

I came across a splendid example of the con-man at work a few years ago. A client asked me to take up references on a sales director whom he had appointed as the result of a speculative CV rather than a full-blooded recruitment assignment. The last employer lived in Texas, USA – the president of a very large multinational. I phoned (there was no time for a letter at that stage) his secretary to 'make sure that John Smith wasn't fired for dipping his fingers in the till'. 'Oh, but he was', she said, at which point the great man himself came on the phone and explained that Smith had used his company credit card illegally, had removed cash from another employer and had deserted his (subsequently discovered to be bigamous) wife. 'This man', said the president, 'has caused great grief in dollars.'

Why did John Smith give me this contact as a reference? Because he knew that most companies wouldn't bother to spend £15 on a trans-atlantic phone call.

From the Employer's Viewpoint

From the viewpoint of the employer, the prime purpose of taking up references is, therefore, to check the facts. Only by doing so is it possible to avoid stupid mistakes – as in the case of a chairman of a small company in the West Midlands who unknowingly appointed as his company accountant someone who was on parole following a sentence for fraud.

Note that I talk about 'taking up references', i.e. an active rather than a passive process. It is not good enough merely to see documentary evidence in the form of an open letter. Open references of this nature are valueless and no personnel professional will even wish to look at one. They are too easy to manufacture. A written reference is only valid if it is sent directly and confidentially from the referee to the recruiter or potential employer.

Why does the employer need to check the facts? Because in most cases the only facts known about the candidate are what that candidate has written or said. Too many people take a CV at face value (you may have done so yourself in your last post). When you recruited a new graduate who claimed an upper second, did you confirm this with the university? When you recruited a school-leaver who claimed four GCSEs, did you check with the school or at least see the certificates? Even more to the point, if you have recruited a forty-five-year-old executive who claimed to have been elected a member of a professional institute twenty years ago, did you check with that institute about membership? I doubt it.

If you have been all your working life with one organisation, however large or small, that organisation knows your history. Suppose that you are aged forty-five and have spent twenty-three years with Shell, the Civil Service, Barclay's Bank, the Army or wherever; your personal file has the whole story.

But recruitment normally ain't like that. The only thing that I, as a recruiter, know about a candidate is what I am told. If the CV says 'First-class honours degree in Biosophistry from the University of Steeple Bumpstead' then, as far as I am concerned, the candidate has achieved just that. Naturally I try to use my native cunning at interview to confirm the claim, but broadly I accept it at that stage. Then, when the candidate has been through all the stages and is offered the job subject to references, I take up those references and validate the whole life history.

Timing

Note that in industry and commerce, references should normally be taken up after a conditional offer has been made. To do so earlier would certainly be wrong in the case of a candidate currently in a job, for the word might get around, jeopardising his or her position. Things are often different in the less commercial world, such as the public service and academia. Advertisements for jobs in these areas often ask for the names of three referees to accompany the application.

Written v Phoned References

To establish the facts with surety, something in writing is required. So the employer (or personnel department or recruitment consultant) should write to the referees. My letter would go something like this:

> Dear Mr Rivington-Jones
>
> My client, the chairman of Westshire Widgets Ltd, has offered (subject to satisfactory references) the appointment of managing director to Mr Jasper Wortlebury. Mr Wortlebury has given me your name as one of his referees.
>
> I would be most grateful if you would:
> a. Confirm that Mr Wortlebury worked for you at Plastic Components Ltd during the period mid-1985 to December 1989, his final appointment being that of sales director.
> b. Say if you know of any reason why the appointment should not be confirmed.
>
> Yours sincerely

The point is, if Wortlebury was fired, let's say for feeding key product information to competitors, Rivington-Jones is going to be unenthusiastic about making the categorical statement in writing that 'I know of no reason why the appointment should not be confirmed'. Instead I may receive a quiet phone call from Rivington-Jones saying that he is not prepared to write such a letter.

What usually happens, when there are no skeletons, is that Rivington-Jones sends a letter following the suggested line, but adding his own assessment of Wortlebury. That is generally enough to tick off that reference as OK, and all that is required is a letter of thanks. If, however, there is something in the letter which sounds a discordant note, a telephone call will usually clarify the issue — it was either a hurried piece of dictation, which raised unnecessary doubts, or a carefully worded note of warning.

At this stage I also check the facts on qualifications. Normally it is possible to do this by phoning the university or professional body. This call is usually welcome, for it is in the interest of the organisation concerned to ensure that its standards are not claimed undeservedly.

As usual, there are major cultural differences in different countries. In some it is practically illegal to do any checking, which presumably creates an attractive environment for con-men.

Adverse References

This process must be handled with care by the recruiter, as it can lead to the law courts. Thus there is some advantage to the employer if the recruiter is able to do some checking prior to short-list, in which case a candidate who has been rubbished by one or more referees can be rejected at short-list in favour of someone else, rather than later purely on the grounds of references.

Referees from Your Viewpoint

How do you manage your affairs in order to respond to the needs of a potential employer to verify your background?

Assuming you are now out of work, the first thing to do is to establish what your last employer (Mr Hyde) will say. You will recall that we discussed this in chapter 5.

Your aim at the time was to part on a friendly basis. If Mr Hyde is likely to be difficult (the worst case situation), you should consider using somebody reliable who knows of your work while you were under Mr Hyde. For example, supposing you are an accountant who had personality problems with Mr Hyde because you would not bend the rules on his behalf, you might ask the firm's auditor to act as a reference for you. One can think of other similar cases, such as a major customer if you were in a sales appointment. If the worst comes to the worst, you might consider leaning on Mr Hyde in order to avoid a poor reference, but I suggest you consult a lawyer first, referring him for starters to Spring *v* Guardian Assurance plc (*The Times* Law Report 10 February 1992 [QB]).

Additionally, you need as referees a number of earlier bosses – either within the corporation, if you have been a one-company person, or from the various companies for which you have worked. On the list should also be an ex-subordinate; if you are any good, there will be someone who has worked for you who would be very supportive and this sometimes goes down frightfully well with potential employers (probably more so than with professional recruiters).

If you are at an early stage in your career and have little employment experience, you should include people who know your work, such as school-teachers, university tutors and employers during vacation jobs.

It is wise also to include a personal referee, someone of standing who has known you for a long time and who can vouch for the overall story of your life. By 'of standing' I am not suggesting that you should start name-dropping; candidates who think they need to do so are both obvious and pretty nauseating. I am thinking rather of someone like your family's lawyer, a former school or university friend who is now a doctor, accountant or something similar. Recruiters tend not to take up personal references, but it is useful to have one in reserve if needed.

Then write (or phone, if appropriate) to them all, asking them if they would be so kind as to act as referees on your behalf and if they are prepared to take phone calls as well as receive letters. When all have agreed, produce a list of the referees, with names, addresses and phone numbers (if applicable) on the left and the connection (e.g. 'My Manager at XYZ Ltd 1983–1987') on the right, opposite each name. Head the list with your request that approaches should be made only with your agreement. Then, when asked, you can offer the list and agree with your interlocutor which referees are appropriate in the particular instance.

Additionally, you should carry a dossier of certificates and photocopies thereof. In my chapter on interviewing (Eyeball to Eyeball) I will discuss exactly how to use them.

Assuming that you are unemployed, you can offer references at an early stage, making it very clear that you do not want the referees to be approached without clearance on each occasion. Provided this is done reasonably and professionally, it should not raise hackles. Orally (i.e. on the telephone or at an interview) you can make the point that 'being a professional in this business you will, of course, appreciate that I would like to forewarn any referees you want to approach – they are all being inundated and I would not wish to upset them'. A similar message at the top of any list should do the trick.

Brief Your Referees

If this works, you will have an opportunity to brief your referees before each approach. Ostensibly, this will be purely a matter of courtesy to warn them to expect telephone calls or letters. In fact, your aim in this forewarning is more devious, in that you can ask the referee to focus on any particularly relevant issue. If, for example, you are in the running for a job in which extensive travel is necessary and the potential employer feels that you may be too old for the stress of travel, get your referees to emphasise your dynamism and love of rushing about in all directions in aeroplanes.

For they probably will be asked about your suitability for the job in addition to being asked to confirm the facts. I feel this can be taken too far, as the referee does not personally know the potential employer or the company you may be joining, so can have relatively little idea as to whether or not you are suitable. However, since potential employers and recruitment professionals do often ask such questions, it makes sense for you to turn such activity to your advantage.

To summarise:
* Your reference from your last employer is critical. Make every effort to ensure that this will not torpedo your chances.
* Prepare a list of referees, whose permission must naturally be sought, to cover all aspects of your working life.
* Do your best to ensure that no referee will be approached until you have agreed on each occasion (this may prove difficult).
* Whenever possible, brief referees about an impending approach, using the opportunity to emphasise characteristics relevant to that appointment.

9

Up the Organisation

'Good order is the foundation of all good things'
EDMUND BURKE

The Loneliness of the Long Distance Job-hunter

If you have been accustomed to working within a well-organised administrative structure, with secretaries, receptionists, telephonists, accountants, telephones, faxes, teleprinters, photocopiers, etc. to manage the minutiae of your working life, you are going to find it something of a shock now you are job-hunting on your own. You need to set up your own office and your own administrative systems.

If you are starting out on your working career or are at an early stage in it, the shock will be less severe, in that you will never have enjoyed much – if any – of the administrative conveniences referred to above. (No, don't give me a hard time about referring to people as administrative conveniences, you know perfectly well what I mean.) But if you are, say, a student about to graduate or leave school, you will at least have had a careers organisation to call on for some assistance.

In this chapter I am not going to produce detailed instructions on how to set up your administration, first because I'd probably omit something and secondly because you will have your own ideas about how to manage your job-hunt. Let's just consider some aspects.

Equipment and Your Office

The first thing to do is to establish your office. Ideally this will be your own room, where you can work without interruption, but we don't live in an ideal world. You may have to compromise and your room may become your corner of a room also used by others.

Wherever you work, you must have a phone beside you and you must be able to conduct phone business in a businesslike way. If your only phone is in the living-room, which is often buzzing with television and/or hi-fi, you've got a problem. One solution is to buy a walk-about phone. I realise that this is adding cost at a moment when you are, understandably, panicking about money, so the support and discipline of those around you may have to be your fall-back position.

Answerphone, Fax and Photocopier

I have already said that you need an answerphone. If you can get one with an integrated fax machine, so much the better. If not, you may have a nearby bureau or secretarial services office which you could use for sending and receiving faxes. Better still, again because you must minimise cost, find a friend or neighbour who has a fax and do a deal to pay for just the actual cost of the phone calls, plus a bottle of lemonade or something stronger when you have got your job.

The same considerations apply to finding a photocopier for your use.

Typing and the Dreaded PC

The next thing you must sort out is typing. If you have not got this facility in-house (and this means *your* house), you must look elsewhere. There are plenty of secretarial agencies around. Better still, possibly, there are many highly competent women with good typewriters and/or word processors who are bringing up a family and who would like to supplement the family income (and, just as importantly, put a little extra interest into their lives) by working from home. Try *Yellow Pages*, local directories, the classified columns of the local press, the newsagent's window or ask around (i.e. network the search).

If you have your own PC or word processor, this problem is solved. However, please don't become wedded to it so that you are incapable of planning or doing anything unless you are sitting in your office-at-home with your fingers rippling over the keyboard. I have in mind one patient of mine who, when he came to see me for counselling sessions, never knew what he had done, what he was going to do or what progress he was making on specific tasks because 'it's all on the computer at home'. For example, you should not (whatever elegant software you have) keep your diary on your computer. As we shall see when we discuss interviews and networking meetings, it is essential to be able to diarise appointments on the spot rather than have to rush home to the computer.

'But', I hear you cry, 'these are the 1990s. Why can't I bring along my laptop and agree appointments using that?' Certainly that might be a good idea when visiting young, dynamic, hi-tech companies, but I would not recommend it for all your meetings. Therefore you will have to use a good old-fashioned diary much of the time, and you cannot keep half the information on a computer and half in the diary, lest you double book.

Records

You will have to open a series of records so that you know where each project has got to and whom you have seen. You can devise your own, I am sure. The record for responses to advertisements will have columns such as:

Serial No
Date of advt
Source of advt
Advertiser
Job
Job Ref.
Date of application
Date of receipt of acknowledgement
Date of 1st interview
and so on.

When you have read the chapter on networking, you will readily be able to devise a suitable system to track your path through the network.

If you are really well organised, you might consider keeping a master alphabetical list of all the people you meet, write to, talk to on the telephone and hear talked about during your job search. (Your PC would certainly come in useful here.) You will find − particularly if you work in a specialised area − that names often crop up more than once and your networking will gain an extra dimension of sophistication if you really know who's who and can make appropriate connections.

Business Cards

In chapter 5 I suggested that you should have get some simple cards made – handing them out will assuredly bring some in return.

Let me pass on a tip which I was given about ten years ago and which I have found to be invaluable. Most people keep cards in alphabetical order. Why? If you can remember the name of the person whose card you are seeking, you can probably find the card by a quick search through your card book or find the information you seek (e.g. phone number, address) via other means. Much more often you want to find the card of someone you met, but whose name you can't remember. Perhaps you say to yourself: 'I really ought to talk to that chap I met at the Institute's regional dinner last autumn.' What you can remember is when you met him, rather than his name. So I advise you to store cards in date order of receiving them, pencilling the date on the card before you slot it into your card book.

Note that I recommend one of these storage books with transparent slots, rather than a card index system. Going through the latter is a laborious and time-consuming task, whereas scanning pages is relatively painless.

A Real Office

A proper office? If you have been given outplacement counselling with an office near your home, you may be able to use that as your main office – though you will inevitably have to work from home a certain amount. If you are really lucky, your previous life support systems may be available for a period, which will make your administration a whole lot easier. I have in mind, for example, the announcement in June 1992 of the imminent closure of the offices of Neddy (the National Economic Development Council). The office did not actually close until 31 December 1992, so the staff were able to use all the offices' resources for six months. If you can swing that kind of support from your previous employer, you really have cracked the organisation problem.

To summarise:
* You must set up your own administrative organisation to support your campaign.
* Do as much as you can to provide yourself with a telephone you can use in peace and quiet, an answerphone, a fax system and a photocopier – without spending money, if possible.

* If you have your own typing equipment, well and good. If not, establish reliable secretarial support.
* Keep meticulous records, so that you are in control of your own job search.
* Collect business cards assiduously and keep them in date order.
* If circumstances permit, consider asking for office support from your previous employer.

10

Your CV

'Our deeds still travel with us from afar
And what we have been makes us what we are.'
GEORGE ELIOT

Thumbs Down to Standard CVs

This chapter may be a great disappointment to you. It is not going to show you what the perfect CV looks like so that you can copy it, merely replacing the sample's details with your own. There is no such thing as a perfect CV which applies to everyone – only a good CV that applies to you.

You should know that the recruiter's heart sinks when yet another standard format CV appears. We can all recognise a CV produced for a patient of one of the big outplacement firms or, on a more local level, a CV produced for, say, a college-leaver which is exactly the same as all the other college-leavers' CVs, because one CV-producing firm has cornered the local market. No personality comes through: just pre-packaged, sanitised, characterless verbiage.

The layout must depend on your life history. If, for example, you have worked for one company for many years, serving in many different countries and speaking many different languages, you may decide that the image – the snap-shot – you wish to create, in that critical thirty seconds, is one of loyalty combined with variety of international experience. If, on the other hand, you have changed employers many times and worked in different disciplines, you may wish to sell yourself as someone who will bring wide functional experience to the new employer. These two images need different treatment.

My experience is that the best CVs are those whose initial draft has been written by someone who has not been tutored in the art and who has not looked at examples. Indeed, that is an exercise you should now undertake. Sit down and write your CV. If you took my advice earlier, you will have an autobiography which will be of great use here. Don't worry that your first CV will look nothing like your final one. By producing a first draft untrammelled by preconceptions, you will eventually have a better CV than if you slavishly copy examples.

This chapter will explain in some detail how to go about the task of drafting your CV, and what factors you should consider in designing the layout. Then read on, having produced that first draft.

What Is a CV?

CV stands for *curriculum vitae*, which might be translated as 'the course of one's life'. Just think of it as a brief life history. Indeed, it is sometimes referred to as such. Other synonyms used are *'résumé'* and 'career summary'. I suggest you stick to CV. (Some people try to show off by referring to their *curriculum vitae* and treating it as plural, e.g. '... my curriculum vitae are ...', thereby proving that a little knowledge is a dangerous thing.)

All those in and around the recruitment scene – candidates, personnel managers, professional recruiters, outplacement counsellors, CV-producing firms – have strong views on CVs and yours will not satisfy everyone. But by thinking the matter through, you should be able to bring the greatest happiness to the greatest number. Let us start by considering some fundamentals before we get down to detail.

The Aim

Remember the aim of the CV. It is: *to get an interview*. There is a secondary aim which you must meet in order to achieve that main aim; this is: *to be read properly – i.e. to pass the 30-second filter and to be put on the pile to be read again.*

This secondary aim is most important when you are one of six hundred applicants replying to an advertisement. It is obviously far less important if, for example, a managing director asks you to send him your CV as a result of a networking contact. If he has asked for it, you can make the *prima facie* assumption that he will read it.

The deduction from this is that your CV should be attractive, brief, clear, factual and have sex appeal.

Look Before You Read

Consider the glaringly-obvious-but-frequently-forgotten fact that no one ever reads anything without looking at it first. You want your target to read your CV in a positive frame of mind. If it looks good, your chances of achieving that are increased.

Brevity

There is so much evidence in favour of short CVs it astonishes me that people still churn out pages and pages of the stuff. Every time I see the results of a survey on the topic I make a note: 91% prefer between one and three pages; 73% prefer two or three pages; and so on. Personally I think that two pages are quite sufficient, bearing in mind the primary and secondary aims. If you should meet someone in favour of four-five- or six-page CVs, gently enquire about the purpose of the document. I'll bet you receive the usual nonsense about 'it's to describe myself' or 'it's the summary of my career'. Don't take the bet; you'll lose.

If you insist on going to three pages, then do so. You won't have my blessing, but we'll stay friends. But four or more – goodbye.

There are exceptions to this. You may feel you need a more comprehensive document for certain purposes or your employment posture may be such that more detail is expected – for example, university teachers produce long lists of their published papers. My advice is that you can produce as long a career history as you like as a second CV, but never send it or give it to anyone unless asked so to do. For example, some interviewers do like detailed papers to work from, and there is nothing to stop you phoning before an interview or meeting to say, 'I do have a more detailed career history – would you like me to send it to you before our meeting?' If the interviewer likes such things, you will earn additional gold stars before the meeting. If not, your call has done no harm.

Graduates and School-Leavers

If you are at the beginning of your working career, say a new graduate or a school-leaver, one page is quite sufficient. This page should include four ingredients. First, the basic personal facts. Secondly, details of education. Thirdly, details of any holiday or vacation jobs you have had, thus demonstrating that you are not just a TV moron. And finally, enough about your interests and experiences to make you appear to be that little bit different from your contemporaries.

Incidentally, I believe that everyone should prepare a CV for the first time at the age of fifteen or sixteen and build it up thereafter. If you make your first draft later – say in your final year at university – you will probably have forgotten about some of the more interesting things you did when younger.

Clarity

If I were to pick one common characteristic in CVs which causes me to jump up and down and throw things against the wall, it would be the lack of clarity. A common example will make the point. Take a career summary:

Career Summary

1991–present	INTERNATIONAL SALES MANAGER	bloggs plc
1989–91	FAR EAST SALES MANAGER	Chan Tao pty
1986–89	MARKETING MANAGER	bloggs plc
1983–86	OPERATIONS MANAGER (USA)	Appleheimer & bloggs inc
1980–83	SALES MANAGER, EUROPE	bloggs plc

Remember, I've got thirty seconds. I look at this and see that the person perpetrating this CV has a wavelength of two to three years and never settles in any job. A closer look would disclose that this summary shows steady and honourable progression – even Chan Tao pty is a wholly-owned subsidiary of the bloggs plc group. Yes, of course it's accurate – but the layout does not help me. You would be surprised how much time it can take to work out the true movement pattern – and that time is just not available.

The Facts

When I pick up your CV, I know little or nothing about you. Little, if it has reached me under cover of a letter – and to my mind the letter is the critical document which affects the way in which I tune into your CV. Nothing, if it has been passed to me – say by a mutual contact through networking – or has been sent to me under a compliments slip. So what I want is fact. More and more people are producing CVs which start thus:

PROFILE

A dynamic and pragmatic operations manager who combines vision, exceptional leadership skills, wisdom and an overwhelming modesty ...

Lest you think that my imagination is overtaking reality, here are two examples which have recently crossed my desk. They are both quoted verbatim, as there are no details which might identify the perpetrators of these gems:

PROFILE

An experienced talented professional with a highly successful track record. A commercially aware accomplished manager with proven motivational and man management skills. A proven strategist and innovator with extensive sales and marketing skills proven in home and international markets. An accomplished negotiator and experienced manufacturing manager and engineer.

The gentleman doth protest too much, methinks. But he is put in the shade by my second example:

PROFILE

A computer literate, team orientated, 'Hands On' engineering management professional, with excellent communication skills. Well versed in, and committed to, contemporary manufacturing techniques, exemplified by Concurrent Engineering, Design for Manufacture, TQM, FMEA, SPC, MRP, JIT, Kanban, TOPS, Yokeru Poka and Taguchi, within the framework of BS5750, ISO9000, AQAP and Ford Quality standards; fused with the financial abilities, cost reduction analysis skills and commercial astuteness, necessary in todays' modern competitive industry and global marketplace. Whose career history to date includes strategy planning, implementing and managing necessary significant and complex changes to production processes, contract estimating and tendering, high value capital plant justification, procurement, and, developing and introducing effective IT systems, with full profit and loss responsibilities within unionised environments. Who has extensive experience in, and an in-depth knowledge of, product design and development, project management, manufacturing, maintenance scheduling and practices, production engineering, production control, quality engineering and process automation encompassing the fabrication, machining and assembly of mechanical, hydraulic and electrical modules within the Aerospace, Armament, Automotive, Defense and Shipbuilding Industries, in both OEM and sub-contract environs utilising advanced manufacturing technologies.

I am not alone in this reaction to such self-portraits. Some time ago I

was discussing the whole question of CVs with some friends and
Brenda Bruce, who had recently been involved in a recruitment operation for a charity she supports, subsequently (having been subjected to
assault by CV) wrote to me thus:

> 'Having recently surfaced from a spate of selecting and inter-
> viewing for a post at a voluntary organisation of which I am
> chairman, I am trading on our long acquaintance to ask what
> you honestly think about the current vogue for providing a
> prospective employer with a *curriculum vitae*.
>
> Although I am referring to a small concern, (set up some
> years ago to provide supplementary help for elderly and
> handicapped people and their carers), it is as important to us
> as to an industrial giant to select the right person for the jobs
> we offer.
>
> I am not opposed to CVs *per se*, but feel I am becoming
> increasingly cynical about them. The more of them I see, the
> more I regard them as tools of moderate worth, put together
> prettily by a job applicant and a word processor, to a formula
> taught as part of a business studies course. Why otherwise do
> they all pronounce their authors as being dedicated people,
> hard working, good mixers and with senses of humour?

American Influence?

Perhaps one of the reasons this style of self-adulatory CV is seen
increasingly in the UK is that much of the accepted doctrine on job-
hunting is of American origin, not least through some of the big
outplacement firms. One cannot ignore the fact that there is a cultural
gap the width of the Atlantic.

For example, when my daughter moved to Florida, she found that
she had to reword her CV so as to emphasise her talents in a more
forthright fashion. And this is not only a British perception. Some time
ago I found myself interviewing a Frenchman for a job in the UK. I
was particularly interested in one part of his career history, when he
set up a subsidiary in Texas on a green-field site. When I asked him
what surprised him most about the cultural change, he said that he was
accustomed to the French (which he then changed, tactfully, to the
European) approach in which people admit only to those skills they
actually have, whereas Americans claim to be able to do anything, but
in most cases can't unless they have 'the procedure' to hand. However,
I feel that the common language makes the cultural difference between
the British and Americans particularly significant. In his brilliant book
on the Korean War, Max Hastings illustrates the point neatly:

> Some of those most intimately concerned with the Imjin battle
> believed that it revealed the fatal disadvantages of committing
> an independent national brigade group in a major war. Briga-
> dier Tom Brodie found himself bearing the brunt of an assault
> by two Chinese divisions, with important implications for the
> safety of Seoul. Yet as a British officer under temporary
> American command, he could not be expected to achieve the
> clear understanding with higher formations that would have
> been possible with his own fellow-countrymen. A British
> officer at Brigade HQ believed that the Americans did not
> understand until much too late how desperate was the predica-
> ment of 29 Brigade: 'When Tom told Corps that his position
> was "a bit sticky", they simply did not grasp that in British
> Army parlance, that meant "critical". Brodie was twice told by
> American Corps headquarters that he could not withdraw his
> brigade, and he felt that he had no choice but to obey.'

The moral of all this is that you should be prepared to break my rule
about having only one CV if you are approaching American firms, in
which case you may have to have a special transatlantic version.

As a footnote to these thoughts, I must emphasise that this is in no
sense an anti-American diatribe. In suggesting that there is a difference,
I am not arguing that one approach is superior to the other.

Quantify

As part of the factual approach, it is essential to quantify. It is not
enough to say: 'Successfully recruited, trained and managed the European sales force'. That might mean anything. To start with, what does
'successfully' mean? Nor do we want the 'aren't I wonderful?' approach,
on the lines of:

> Masterminded growth in Europe, recruiting and training an
> excellent sales force and providing leadership of such remark-
> able quality that the Chairman himself gave me lunch at his
> club.

How much better to provide some feeling for the scope of the
activity:

> Increased European sales from £700K to £5.4M over 4 years.
> This required recruiting, training and managing a team of 4
> sales executives and 3 support staff.

Some advisers say you should now explain how you achieved this,
but I don't necessarily agree. First because the CV will quickly grow

to four, five or more pages. Secondly because those facts are enough to interest me. When I interview you, I shall surely ask you about the situation when you took on the job, how you went about the task, the reasons for your success and what you would do differently with the benefit of hindsight. With luck, the interview will focus on this success story – which is just the sort of focus you are hoping for. If, however, you tell me exactly how you did it, I shall not be bursting to ask you. So don't give everything away in your CV – but give it enough factual content to make me want to hear more.

Sex Appeal

By sex appeal I mean that magic ingredient that makes you, the subject of the CV, seem a little bit different from and a little bit more interesting than the next candidate.

What you have to put into the CV to achieve that reaction is hard to say. I can think of examples, however. I once made a marginal decision to interview a chap who had taken a year out between school and university, hitch-hiked to India and sat at the feet of a guru for six months, visiting Nepal for good measure. And another person who had got into Tibet when it was exceptionally difficult to do so. Then there was the woman who had just returned from two years in a senior executive appointment in Japan; her CV made enough mention (but no more) to interest me in the problems of working at this level in a male-dominated environment.

These examples relate to travel, perhaps because I believe that people who have seen something of the world have more to offer than the stay-at-homes, but there are many other ways of being that little bit special, that little bit more interesting. I'd be fascinated to meet someone who had climbed the Matterhorn, written a symphony, adopted a manatee, exhibited at the Royal Academy, played chess against Nigel Short or Bobby Fischer, been down the Cresta Run, started a school, planted a vineyard ... The possibilities are endless.

'Hold on', you say, 'how can I claim to be any of these things? I am an ordinary, hard-working citizen seeking a job.' Nonsense – you are special, you are different, you are unique and, above all, you are interesting. If you can't convince yourself of this, then a brain-storming session with your counsellor should unearth something that makes you that little bit different.

Don't misunderstand me over this. If I, as a recruiter, am looking for a civil engineer who speaks fluent Spanish, you can have written half a

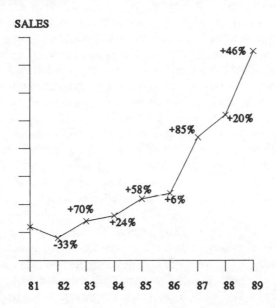

dozen symphonies and climbed Everest with a gas stove on your head, but, if you are not a civil engineer who speaks fluent Spanish then you don't obtain an interview.

You might, for example, use illustrations on the grounds that a picture's worth a thousand words. By this I do not mean cartoons (humour should be avoided in a CV) or photographs, but perhaps a small graph or bar chart to indicate some measurable achievement might work. The above graph, for example, was the one which I put in my CV to show the progress of the HR consultancy I grew with 3i.

Don't go overboard about this. All I'm saying is that, when you're on the margin, you stand a better chance of obtaining that critical interview if you stand out as being that little bit more interesting than the next candidate.

One CV or Many?

You must now decide if you will produce one CV, for use with every approach, or if you will produce a one-off special for each requirement. The latter course is relatively easy if you own or have access to a word processor. But I do not recommend it.

Apart from the fact that it is confusing, you are never sure where any CV will finish up. If one of your network contacts asks for half a dozen copies, you can hardly enquire about the likely destination of each one in order to provide six tailor-made versions. Your CV will be widely circulated and it must cover all eventualities.

Your CV is a selling document and has no value if it is not seen. Some years ago I went on a course about job-hunting. The lecturer said, 'If you go into a public lavatory and find that someone has written "Kilroy was here" on the wall in chalk, get out your own piece of chalk, add "and here's his CV" and then stick your CV to the wall with chewing-gum.' I am not suggesting you should start chewing gum, but that remark has stayed with me as a vivid illustration of how important it is to get one's CV seen.

Consequently your CV should contain key words to cover all your experience and all opportunities. An example of this. A patient called Bernard Taylor had wide engineering experience and in his CV he included, in punchy, one-word mentions, many aspects of engineering of which he had some experience, but which were outside his mainstream appointments. One copy of his CV went through several hands and eventually struck oil because just one of these words rang a bell with a potential employer. If he had produced a special CV for the original recipient that word would not have been included.

So your CV should be universal, at least for the United Kingdom. I have already suggested that you might make an exception to this rule when playing the transatlantic card. You might also consider having your CV translated into the appropriate language if applying for a job (either in the UK or elsewhere) in a foreign company. (A case was reported in the press of someone applying for a job in a Japanese-owned company, who had his CV translated into Japanese and, in due course, got a job.) If you claim fluency in the language in question, you should be able to do the translation yourself. If you can't, you aren't fluent.

Your CV will normally be sent under cover of a letter and you can use that covering letter to emphasise the skills or experience relevant to the job under discussion.

What's in a Name?

Now let's start drafting that CV. At the head of a sheet of A4 you write:

CURRICULUM VITAE

Wrong. I know it's a CV – it has all the visual characteristics of a CV. So don't treat me like an idiot. Try again:

Desdemona Robinson

Much better. Whether or not you put both names or just the surname in capitals, or neither, is up to you. If, however, you are going to include a lot of names, then perhaps that might help, thus:

DESDEMONA Anne Mary ROBINSON

You could put (Miss) or (Mrs) afterwards in parentheses. I can work it out from the personal details below, but your job is to make life easy for me.

There are other ways of indicating the name you use and your initials simultaneously. The American way is:

Gerald T.S. Patworthy

This is a method I have always found hard to take – for absolutely no reason at all. It is, after all, a neat way of packing all the necessary information into a small space. You can help even more by:

Gerald T.S. Patworthy (Gerry)

That's enough on names or we'll never get this CV written.

Personal Details

Next, at the top of the front page and immediately beneath your name, give the basic facts (address, telephone number, etc.). Don't listen to those who tell you to tuck these away at the bottom of page 2. Such people haven't had to screen six hundred CVs in three hundred minutes. Nor should you pay any attention to those who tell you that personal details are optional. I came across this in a book recently. The idea is fatuous, but unfortunately certain bodies have produced guidelines which discourage questions about marital status and age of children. In my opinion it is entirely reasonable to seek a full picture of a candidate, so all personal details help. I was pleased to note that a recent survey showed that 85% of recruiters (personnel managers and consultants) wanted to know about marital status and 55% about age of children. They can't all be idiots.

So you now write down your address, phone number, age and the details of your marital status and family.

Age

Note – age, rather than date of birth.

If you meet, after many years, an old school chum, who reports a marriage and children you don't say, '*What are the dates of birth of your children?*' You say, '*How old are your children?*' If I am carrying out a recruitment, I want to know how old you are, not when you were born (unless of course I am an astrology freak). I am fed up with writing the current year above the date of birth on CVs, and substracting: '*8 from 3 is 5 and carry 1 ...*'. This becomes somewhat exhausting when you have had to do it six hundred times, and bang go those thirty seconds.

But what if your birthday is imminent or if your CV sits on some headhunter's file for a year or two? Your age will then be wrong. So put in the date of birth as an additional piece of information: (born 28 Dec 46) or (dob 28 Dec 46). There is an additional advantage in doing this. One of the most difficult things in job-hunting is to keep in touch with all your contacts. You must keep your name in the frame, but without sounding like a fuss-budget; updating your age is a useful excuse for putting out a new CV.

Telephone Number

If you are job-hunting when you are unemployed, you will probably have only a home number – backed by an answerphone, if you have taken my advice. A fax (possibly integrated with your phone to save the cost of an additional line) would also be an advantage, but that may represent excessive expenditure. However, you may have use of your office for a period, in which case put the office phone number on the CV.

If, on the other hand, you are job-hunting whilst still in a secure job, you must decide whether or not to include your office telephone number. If telephone calls would be unwelcome, leave it out. But if the state of affairs in your office is such that reasonably discreet calls are acceptable, annotate the office phone number with '(with discretion, please)'. If some incompetent search firm does not treat that number with discretion and subsequently gets you fired, sue it.

So the top inch and a half of the first page of your CV might look like this:

Gerald T S Patworthy (Gerry)

Address:	7 Lake Close, Little Sutton, Borsetshire LS9 8TT
Telephone:	0741–339924
Age:	46 (dob 28 Dec 46) Married (2 children: s.22, d.20)

An Overseas Address

If you are currently living overseas, you may have a problem. How much of a problem depends as often as not on the potential employer's industry sector. For example, one client of mine – a major airline – flew a candidate from California to London (and return) for a forty-five-minute interview, all without the flicker of an eyelid. This is rare. An overseas address may shut you out of interviews simply because you present more potential hassle and expense than the next candidate. There may be a case – and I emphasise the word 'may' because it very much depends on circumstances – for using a UK address, either alone or in addition to your overseas address. My son did this when job-hunting from the Army in Germany, putting his German address and telephone number, but adding an additional line immediately under them:

UK Contact: Messages readily passed via David Mackintosh (father).
                [then my address, with home and office phone numbers]

The point of this form of approach is that it sounds helpful. Solving the recruiter's problems, rather than adding to them, is your mission in life.

Another way of helping the recruiter is to say whether or not you can easily get back to the UK for interview – and at whose expense. If this is easy and on a regular basis, you might wish to put something in your CV to the effect that you are regularly back in the UK. If not, your covering letter should, when applying for a job, say something to the effect that you will be back in the UK on leave (or on duty – say which for completeness, but the difference isn't important) during the period X-Y, and that you could make yourself available for interview on certain dates; this will give most recruiters (this one, certainly) a warm glow.

Profile

Now decide if a profile would help – not, of course, a self-adulatory one such as those I have quoted. But it might be useful to write something pithy and factual that gives me, in a few seconds, a snapshot of who you are and where you've come from. Something like:

A PERSONNEL MANAGER who, following an initial grounding in all aspects of personnel work, specialised in pan-European employment law and practice in the hotel, travel and associated leisure industries. Fluent in English, French and Spanish, with some working knowledge of Italian and Norwegian.

If you imagine me sitting down with the pile of CVs, you will agree that a brief profile like this helps me to focus on you. The drawback is that it does type-cast you to some extent, in that you might be screened out for another job you could do perfectly well, because the specification does not match this profile, which has categorised you so precisely.

Do not, however, produce a profile so general that it says nothing at all. That will simply categorise you as a waffler with nothing to say.

Education, Training and Qualifications

The first rule is to concentrate on the final stage of your education, rather than to go into interminable detail about earlier stages. By all means mention your earlier achievements, but don't hammer them into my skull. I remember the husband of a colleague at 3i who came to me for a freebie counselling session. The middle half of the first page of his CV comprised a list of O Levels by subject and grade – about four inches of them. I immediately assumed that this represented the peak of his academic achievement. It was necessary to dig into page 2 (of six!) to discover that he was, in fact, a graduate.

It is obviously easier to be impressively punchy about your academic achievements if you've got an upper second from a decent university and an MBA from Harvard. Don't feel you'll be undervalued if you left school at sixteen and did a five-year apprenticeship. Fortunately there are enough employers who realise that five years on the shop floor usually teaches young people a great deal more about industry than three years at university.

This brings me to training in general. One of the things that surprised me when I left the Army and moved into recruitment was the degree to which candidates would put the shortest and most trivial (in my mistaken view) courses on their CVs: 'Course in time management (1 day)'. I had left off my CV any courses under six weeks long. But I was wrong. Training is expensive and time-consuming, and industrial and commercial companies do not necessarily have the cash or time to spare for their employees to attend lengthy courses. (The whole question of the value of long and short courses is a different matter – potential for another book.) All formal training is worth mentioning, provided you don't make too much of a meal of it. So this section might look like this:

Education, Training and Qualifications

1959–66	Borchester GS (9 × 0; 4 × A)
1966–81	Steeple Bumstead Univ. **BA**(2nd Hons) (economics with pig-keeping)
1981	Heathrow Business School. Senior Management Programme (3 months part-time)
Various	Range of courses (from 2 weeks to 1 day) including principles of management, interviewing, time management, appraisals, finance for non-financial managers, sales.
1983	**CEng MIPE** (Member of the Institute of Patio Engineers)

Note that I have explained the meaning of the initials MIPE, but not BA or CEng. You have to make some assumptions about the street-wisdom of the reader of your CV. For example, I get awfully cheesed off with being told that MBA means Master of Business Administration. I know that. But equally there are some esoteric initials which I don't recognise and a respectful explanation keeps us both happy.

On the subject of superfluous information, do not, repeat *not*, commit the appalling crime which contaminates about 0.5% of the CVs in my mail. This is (and I hope that Carthusians will forgive me for the example) to put:

1957–61   Charterhouse Public School (8 × 0; 3 × A)

If I know Charterhouse is a public school, I don't want to be told. If I don't know, I don't want to be told. Anyway, I don't really care one way or the other (see chapter on prejudice).

The other thing to be wary of is trying to con me by hinting at qualifications which you don't have. It happens a lot, thus:

1961–64   BSc course in astrophysics at Bude University
1966–69   Faringdon Polytechnic course leading to MILM qualification

Both of these entries fill me with grave doubts – implying failure to acquire the appropriate qualification (quite apart from the fact that I don't know what MILM means). So, if you did get that BSc, don't negate your achievement by this sort of wording, which makes me suspect that you are conning me even when you're not.

Avoid bogus qualifications. I came across this the other day:

1979   Graduated as Army Officer

In the real world graduate means get a degree. The Royal Military

Academy at Sandhurst (RMA) does not award degrees. What I object to about 'Graduated as Army Officer' is that it degrades, by embellishment, the real value of RMA training, which is worthwhile in its own right.

Languages

You could also mention your linguistic skills under the education, training and qualifications heading, but I suggest you do so only if you have enough of a foreign language to be worth mentioning, but not enough to make a big thing of it.

If you have really worthwhile language skills, which could be used in your work, put them under a separate heading to emphasise them. On the whole, foreign languages are what the British are worst at. Even though English is now the internationally accepted language in certain sections of industry and commerce, there is unquestionable commercial value to companies in having a few linguists around and thus the language card is worth playing in your CV. (Perhaps I should add that I have no ability in this area, lest you think I am recruiting in my own image, an oft-observed characteristic of everyone involved in the recruitment game.)

If you do mention languages in your CV, help me by making some fairly clear statement of the quality of your expertise. You should readily be able to produce suitably descriptive passages ranging from 'English/French/Spanish (trilingual)' at one end of the spectrum to 'Italian (social use only)' at the other.

Employment Summary

You must now consider whether or not to provide a quick summary of your career — really an employment summary, because it just shows for whom you have worked and for how long. If you have worked for one employer all your working life you will probably make this the first part (and a brief part at that) of your detailed career history, along the lines of:

Career History

1961–present   The Bank of Kingston Lisle plc

Commenced as graduate trainee and subsequently worked in all specialist departments, at home and overseas, progressing to the last two appointments of Vice-President North American Operations and Director Scottish and Arctic Region.

This is the profile under a different guise. It doesn't say a lot — the detail is yet to come. But it gives me that snapshot, the framework in which I can read the detail, the comfort of knowing that I understand the overall picture before I look at the detail. It also contains several useful positive words such as 'progressing'.

More probably you will have changed employer from time to time and the summary will be just a list to give me the feel of where you've been. For example:

Employment Summary

1987-now	Bills & Moon plc	Finance Director
1983–87	Gullane University	Professor of Financial Studies
1965–83	Global Oil plc	Finance Director, Australia (last appt)
1963–65	Smith, Jones, Robinson	Audit Senior
1960–63	McUish, McAish, McTosh	Articled Clerk

I use this as I use the index of a book. It gives me a feeling of knowing where I am — a route card, if you like. And it comforts me.

Note three other things about this summary.

First, it covers your career in reverse order. CVs are always written back to front except for the bit about your education and training. In *Through the Looking-Glass* the Red Queen says: 'It's a poor sort of memory that only works backwards.' She obviously didn't have to read a lot of CVs.

Secondly, I am immediately able to get a feel for your movement pattern. Indeed, I will jot down the following figures on the left of each line, starting at the bottom: '3, 2, 8, 4, 6 + ' these being (roughly) the years you spent with each employer. Thus, when I come to the detail, in which you did five jobs for Global Oil plc in eight years, I will not think that you are the ultimate butterfly who never stops anywhere for very long — but equally, I will know that you are not a stick-in-the-mud.

Thirdly, please, please avoid the perennial attempted con of pretending you are in a job when you're not. In the two examples of employment summaries I have given above, it is clear that the authors are still working for the Bank of Kingston Lisle plc (1961-present) and Bills & Moon plc (1987-now). It is extremely irritating to discover that a candidate who has produced this type of information on a CV left the company concerned eighteen months earlier. It fools no one and is, in any event, pointless. I have already explained that there is no *prima facie* stigma attached to being unemployed, but if you really want to make a recruiter irascible, the attempted con is the way to do so.

We are now half-way down the first page.

Employment History

You now have roughly one and a half pages to describe your work and what you achieved. For each job you must say what it was, what was its scope (quantify) and what you achieved. If you run out of space, concentrate on the later, rather than the earlier, jobs.

Include that touch of sex appeal wherever you can. If you were in charge of a site one thousand miles from your boss, responsible for preparing the case to be put to a parliamentary select committee, the creator of the first advertising campaign on commercial radio or whatever, say so. Describe, quantify and say what you have achieved – modestly but clearly. If you were responsible for gaining a £150M contract to build a ski lift in the Sahara Desert, say so, but don't put it quite like that; say: 'Led the team that ...', which gives a comforting impression of someone who gets the job done, but acknowledges the contribution of others.

If you can, use vivid words and phrases which attract attention and interest, without going over the top. I am nervous about giving examples here, as this part of your CV must represent you and you alone, but I will give one example because it struck me when I saw it – one vivid phrase to focus my attention:

1985–88 **Managing Director, Sanford Sandblasting plc**
         Sanford Sandblasting lost serious money in quarry engineering ...

In all this, avoid use of the word 'I'. If you use it once, you have to use it over and over again. Eventually your CV will look as though it has measles.

Military Matters

Bearing in mind my intention to worst-case-scenario this book, let me return to the Army major with Pain Factor 10 and add a few words about factors special to members of Her Majesty's armed forces who are job-hunting. All the contents of this book apply to servicemen to some degree or another (such as overseas addresses), but there are some special issues. I use the word 'military' to cover all three services.

First is the question of rank. My feeling is that if you have genuinely retired then by all means use your old rank – but if you have genuinely retired, you shouldn't be reading this book. If, however, you wish to embark on a new career, then drop your rank unless you were very important and are being employed for your seniority or are going into a quasi-military appointment. Personally, the only place I am ever addressed as 'Colonel' is at the Blowing Stone Inn in Kingston Lisle – but then everybody needs some identifying sobriquet in a public bar.

The next and more testing difficulty you will find is how to describe your work in terms that the outside world will understand. In this area you will be given conflicting advice, often diametrically opposed. At one extreme you will get the 'civilianise everything' school of thought. Thus if you were the Commanding Officer of the 1st Battalion The Borsetshire Regiment, you are told to describe yourself as the Managing Director. Rubbish! I agree that directors sitting round the boardroom table are probably no longer battle-scarred veterans of the Second World War, but I suggest that recent events in the Falklands, Kuwait and the Balkans, to say nothing of Northern Ireland and any other little local difficulties which have erupted by the time you read this, have resulted in most people having some idea of what a military commander actually does. So no more managing directors of frigates, please.

What you must do, however, is quantify and explain. Quantify in terms of total workforce, the capital cost of equipment, the annual running costs of the whole set-up, etc.

At the other end of the spectrum are those people who believe, deep down, that everyone in the recruitment world should be able to understand military jargon. This just won't do. In my last job in the Army I was, as it happens, GS01(W), GS(OR)6, ACGS(OR), MOD(A). Anyone in the system knew exactly what I did (or purported to do) and could have written my job description without prompting, but it is gibberish to anyone else. Therefore jobs away from the easily understood military activities, such as driving ships or aeroplanes or patrolling Belfast, need a clear, factual and quantified brief description. This should not be too difficult, because staff appointments and administrative jobs relate more readily to civilian jobs.

More difficult is the fact that military CVs can become repetitive – boringly so – if you have done similar jobs at ever increasingly senior levels. If you feel this to be a danger, you might, alternatively, describe your employment history under functional headings rather than chronologically. Separate headings for line management, personnel, training, project management, administration and so on are the sort of thing I have in mind.

Don't think that you have nothing to offer. First, you have been trained properly. Don't write long descriptions of the courses you have been on, however; one line on significant courses will suffice, in the way described earlier in this chapter. Other courses can be lumped together in a portmanteau paragraph, with lots of juicy key words to intrigue. Try this:

Range of courses (from 7 months to 1 day) including general
management and specialist (eg human behaviour, interviewing, account-
ing, auditing, law, computer modelling, strategic planning, social styles).

Secondly, you have probably achieved much more than you believe
– though if you wrote a suitably immodest autobiography some
chapters ago, you'll have overcome that hurdle. You may have operated
at the end of a long line without much in the way of life support
systems. Or you may have been responsible for relocating a large
chunk of the taxpayers' resources – hundreds of servicemen and
servicewomen and their dependants, thousands of tons of equipment
including some very dangerous stuff – across countries or continents.
You may have learnt some quite important lessons about, and made a
significant contribution to, the business of government at the highest
level. And your presentation skills should be sufficiently tuned to put
all this over to a recruiter or a potential employer.

The Magnificent Seven

One final point about listing achievements (or anything else for that
matter). Never produce a list of more than seven points.

I am told by experts that the short-term memory favours a limit of
seven. If you think of it, the number seven is pretty important in our
lives. We think of seven seas, continents, days in the week, dwarfs,
deadly sins, brides for brothers, fat kine, veils, ages of man, samurai,
year itch, wonders of the world, pillars of wisdom, league boots, sages,
maids with mops; and above all, we have Joshua with seven priests
bearing seven trumpets compassing Jericho seven times on the seventh
day and, as the song says, 'the walls came tumbling down'.

Whether or not there is some deep scientific reason for all this, the fact
is that whenever I see a list with more than seven items in it my mind
starts to wander. Equally, if I am examining the structure of a
company and find any manager has more than seven people report-
ing directly to him or her, I have grave doubts about the wisdom
of such an organisation.

So, when you make a list – for example of achievements in your
latest or most significant job – don't include more than seven items,
and preferably fewer. I would rather read about three or four really
important things you have achieved than a dozen or more which
merely leave me further confused.

Leisure Interests

By the time you have described your job and listed your achievements you will be on to page 4. So you will now go back and edit what you have written, honing it to a punchy, clear, quantified story of progress and achievement. It will still be over two pages, but when it is typed, it will be slightly less than two pages, with an inch and a half left at the bottom of page 2 – for your leisure interests?

This is a difficult one. If your leisure interests are 'DIY, gardening and watching TV', don't bother. Nothing wrong with the first two, particularly if you have built your own house or have become a world expert in the breeding of orchids, in which case say so. The trouble is that you don't know what will appeal to the recipient. Some employers respond enthusiastically to 'None – I am wedded to my work,' but, I am glad to report, they are in a minority. Some indication of physical activity is no bad thing (but only put 'jogging' if you aspire to be the President of the United States).

Probably the best list of leisure interests would comprise one each of the following: sporting, artistic/cultural, intellectual, domestic. But what if you don't have such esoteric interests? Then do not, please, make them up – you will surely be found out.

Avoid any suggestion that you have a bee in your bonnet which may make you somewhat exhausting to have around. If you are a part-time politician, for example, you are bound to offend more people than you please once you disclose the party of your choice. Similarly, trade union involvement implies attitudes which may not fit easily into the executive culture. Religion is also a delicate matter. I know that this will upset many people, but when I see 'committed Christian' on a CV I grow nervous. Not that I am against anyone committed to his or her religion, but 'committed' may turn out to mean 'excessively evangelical', and that may not be totally relevant to the workplace.

There are so many conflicting views on the subject that I am not sure it makes much difference. Provided you avoid the really grey topics like 'watching TV', just write what your interests are. When it comes down to it, I want to see, in thirty seconds, if you have the skills and experience to do the job. It will be possible to discover if you will fit into my client's team when I meet you. Then your extra-mural activities may, or may not, prove to be of interest.

Presentation

You gain nothing by presenting your CV in a glitzy fashion with a binder or a folder with transparent sheets over each page and a pompous-looking cover sheet. Most recruiters will pull out the key pages, staple them together and throw away the frippery, so you will have wasted your money. And do not have your CV typed in capital letters throughout – it becomes virtually impossible to read.

Photograph

As with everything about CVs, there is a mix of opinion about attaching a photograph. Personally I am against it – when I interview I'll take a polaroid shot purely as an *aide memoire*. It won't be studio quality stuff, but it will serve its purpose. Overelaborating will probably backfire – like the candidate whose CV I saw recently, which had a photocopy of an A4-size photograph as the front sheet. It looked awful and created only negative thoughts about the owner of the CV.

Variety – the Spice of Life

Lastly, don't feel that you have got to prepare your CV exactly as I have described. There may be valid reasons – your reasons – for changing the sequence, the layout, the way you use words. Good, for the worst CV is one that isn't yours. But do think carefully before ignoring the ideas behind the sort of CV I have proposed.

To summarise:
* Your CV should not exceed two pages of A4, typed; three pages maximum, if you must.
* Do not copy some standard layout – the first draft must be yours.
* Clarity is essential – ask yourself (and your counsellor) if your life history is readily understandable in thirty seconds.
* Describe and quantify throughout.
* Describe achievements rather than boast about them.
* Say enough to interest the recipient without answering all the possible questions.
* Do not employ overelaborate methods of presentation – they are counter productive.

11

Advertisements ... and How to Reply to Them

'I have made this letter longer than usual, only because I have not had time to make it shorter.'

BLAISE PASCAL

Letters Matter

This chapter, and the next one on networking, are the two most important chapters in the book.

Why is this one so important? Because it deals primarily with the writing of letters. Many job-hunters get themselves tied in knots about writing their CVs, which they despatch in all directions under the cover of sloppy, scruffy, illiterate, irrelevant and ill-presented letters. So the CVs never get looked at, let alone read.

It is, however, necessary to discuss the subject of writing letters in context, and I have chosen to do so in the context of replying to advertisements. Not because an advertisement necessarily provides the best chance of getting that job, but because doing so will help both you and me to focus. So let's discuss advertisements first.

The Appointments Pages

Appointments are advertised in the classified pages of the press, which can be divided into national papers, local papers and specialist publications such as magazines, journals and newsletters.

National Newspapers

National newspapers work to a structured programme, with different types of jobs being advertised on different days. At appendix 2 at the end of this book I have listed the most significant national papers for classified advertisements, showing which days they advertise which jobs. I am not suggesting you should buy all the papers which apply to you – you will find them in your friendly library.

Don't feel you must rush out to the library every morning and read the day's output. You have plenty of other things to do with your time and, provided the library keeps the papers for a few days (if you have established the right relationship there, the staff may even keep them for you so you can take them away), you will not lose anything by waiting a few (but not too many) days.

Response Time

This is a convenient moment to discuss the speed with which you should reply to advertisements. If you recall the process as seen from the enemy's trenches, dealt with in chapter 6, you will know that I am not going to start arranging interviews until about ten days after the advertisement has appeared unless the job is very specialised and the response very small. Ideally it is better to submit your application within the first three days, but it will receive its due attention any time in the first ten days.

Don't listen to those who tell you that you should wait for three weeks and then apply. The theory – and it is merely that and not based on experience – is that the recruiter may be tearing his or her hair out by then, as no-one suitable has appeared, so your application will stand out rather than be lost in the wave of paper flooding across the desk. Rubbish. If the response was good, the recruiter feels confident that those applicants already selected for interview will suffice to produce a strong short-list. If the response was poor, the few applicants worth seeing have already been seen. Your response time should never exceed ten days for national newspapers. For weekly newspapers and specialist journals, the response time can be a little longer.

Predated Letters

A word about people who try to con me by predating letters. I have a specific example in front of me: advertisement published 11 February, letter dated 15 February; letter arrives 2 March, postmark reveals letter posted 1 March. (No overseas factor which could explain all this.) The mismatch is either an attempted con or extreme incompetence. Either way, we are unlikely to meet at interview.

Local Press

Whether or not it is worth studying your local press is to some extent a function of the level of job you seek, but not entirely. It also depends on local identity. For example, if you seek work in the London area, you would be foolish to ignore the *Evening Standard*. Certain other parts of the country have strong regional cultures and I have frequently put well-paid senior appointments in local papers – sometimes, but not always, as a back-up to a national campaign. Firms like to advertise locally; it is good PR. Furthermore, the cost of an advertisement in a regional daily or weekly newspaper is markedly less than one in a national newspaper.

You will note that I have included two Scottish papers in my national list at appendix 2, but I could equally have selected regional papers in Wales, the North, the Midlands, the South-West, etc. It is surprising how often job-seekers ignore what is on their doorsteps.

Specialised Press

I cannot even start to list all the specialised publications which may be relevant to your skills and experience. There is a publication called BRAD (British Rate & Data) which lists the vast number of publications which take advertising. BRAD is the bible of all those who advertise, including recruiters. The edition I have in front of me (it is published monthly) lists over seven thousand publications.

Clearly you are not going to read all these. If you are a specialist, either by qualification (e.g. patio engineer) or industry sector (e.g. casinos), you will know which publications to read. But it may be worth spending half an hour with BRAD some time.

Content of Advertisements

A good advertisement describes the organisation or company for which someone is being recruited (unless it is a 'blind' advertisement), the reason for the recruitment exercise, the job to be done, the characteristics of the person sought and the rewards package. It then tells you what to do if you wish to apply. The heading normally emphasises the job title, the location and the benefits.

This sort of advertisement is, therefore, a *précis* of the job specification (the job description plus the employee specification). Some advertisements put the essential points over very well and clearly. If you look at the appointments pages in the quality press, you will see many such clear, helpful advertisements.

You will also see a lot of meaningless rubbish. I have in front of me what is probably the worst advertisement I have ever seen, for a £45K per annum job. Unfortunately I cannot give it in full or I might be sued for libel, but I give here that paragraph which is, I assure you, the only part of the advertisement which deals with the qualifications, experience and characteristics of the person sought:

> '... seeks a Chief Executive to provide active and positive leadership and management in the introduction of a new structure with a focus on performance measures for delivery of a £24 million budget.'

Anyone who can work out from that what the advertiser is seeking is much cleverer than I.

Should You Apply?

Provided you can stand the shock of receiving endless rejection letters – and I am afraid that you must teach yourself to ride the punch – my advice is that, when in doubt, you should apply. Don't waste time and money on clear NOGOs; unless you are qualified, you will not get that job as a brain surgeon.

One way to overcome the pain of rejection is to treat every rejection letter as a step on the road to success. If, for example, you hope to score one interview for every thirty applications, then statistically you should get one interview for every twenty-nine rejections, and ten interviews for every two hundred and ninety rejections. You will not maintain your success percentage if you apply for really hopeless NOGO jobs, but, within sensible limits, the number of successes will grow alongside rejections. This method is often used to motivate telephone sales staff, who can have a pretty miserable life without something to make their jobs more interesting.

How to Apply

If you decide to apply, follow the instructions contained in the advertisement. Normally you are asked to apply in writing, enclosing your CV. If so, it is pointless to write without a CV.

Instructions may be more specific. You may be asked to include, for example, salary history or a list of languages in which you would be prepared to be interviewed. In which case, do so. Some advertisements ask you to telephone, others to fax your CV. Whatever the advertisement calls for, comply. Unless you are overseas, in which case the rules can be modified, don't use the fax unless asked. Always follow up fax with hard copy.

Should your letter be typed or handwritten? Preferably typed; it is much easier for the recipient to read a typed letter fast than a handwritten one. Naturally, you will reply in manuscript if the advertisement asks you to do so. (This may mean that your letter will be scrutinised by an amateur or professional graphologist.)

Stamp your envelope – do not use your company's franking machine (this obviously applies only if you are still in work). Use of the company's franking machine suggests, possibly unfairly, theft. Normally a second-class stamp will do, unless you are somewhat late in replying or unless you may miss the closing date for applications, if one is indicated in the advertisement.

Application Forms

Sometimes advertisements ask you to phone or write for an application form. In which case, do so – don't at this stage waste time writing a letter explaining why you should have the job.

Application forms are a pain in the neck for candidates. They take time to complete properly – time which may be wasted if you are to be screened out instantly. Helpful recruitment systems will ask you to fill in a form only if and when you have crossed the first (screening) hurdle. Then at least you know that you have an interview and the laborious business of completing that form will not be entirely wasted.

There are two simple rules for completing application forms.

First, photocopy it and complete the photocopied form to your satisfaction before filling in the original with care. It is an inexorable law of nature that anyone completing any substantial form makes mistakes – usually because of bad design.

The second rule is to avoid continuation sheets, even if you are invited to use them if you wish. If the form has a box the width of an A4 page and, say, 15 cm deep in which you are invited to write about your career aspirations, you should use that space and no other. If you go on to continuation sheets you are in effect saying, 'This is a badly-designed form as you haven't given me enough space for this item.'

Do you type or write? Typing information into small boxes is time-consuming and prone to error, so write the details in, but in your

Sunday best writing. The larger boxes need thought. Typing allows you to put more information or discussion into the box, and is easier to read. But the recipient will probably guess that you are doing this because your handwriting is poor. My answer is this: if your handwriting is legible, complete the whole form by hand; if it is as illegible as mine, complete the small boxes carefully by hand and type the contents of the larger discussion-type boxes.

Should you enclose your CV? Yes, but don't write 'See CV' all over the form unless you are specifically invited to do so.

Return the application form with a covering letter, just as you do when replying to a letter with CV advertisement. That letter is of vital importance and for the rest of this chapter we will consider what makes a good – and a bad – letter of application.

The Aim

What follows is specifically directed at letters written in response to advertisements, but most of it applies to letters generally.

Let us start by defining the aim of a letter in response to an advertisement. The aim of a letter of this nature is to obtain an interview – or at least to get the recruiter to read your CV and then select you for interview.

I am now going to be pretty rude about illiteracy levels and you may not like or want to hear it. How you write letters to your spouse, parents, children, friends, relatives, lovers, significant partners or bank manager is no concern of mine. But you want a job, and if you can produce the right sort of letter, you will increase your chances of an interview by a significant factor. My job is to help you to do so.

Some Examples of Gibberish

Please don't think that I'm riding a tiresome hobby-horse of no significance. Every day I receive letters seeking jobs or advice and my mind boggles, as yours would, at the illiterate gibberish which is meant to pass for communication. Let me give you two examples.

First, a twenty-nine-year-old honours graduate (electronic and electrical engineering) wrote to me, following a telephone interview, as follows:

> Dear David,
> following our recent telephone convisation plese find my CV
> enclosed (this is fairly recent) ...

But why should we blame him? Why do we expect the young to write reasonable English if their elders are incapable of doing so? Here is one sentence (yes, one sentence) of a letter which I received recently from the chief executive of one of the 88 TECs. For obvious reasons I have changed the geographical details:

> We are sorry that you will not become a registered Investors in People Advisor at this point in time,as we believe that there will be considerable benefits in other fields resulting from the Investors in People programme and we as a company will be looking to our associate advisors' as the first point of call for other business consultancy services which will be required throughout the county and the region and our objective over the next six months is to build special relationships with our associate advisors' so that we can establish the appropriate quality contols on the work we will do together and then to use the associate advisor network as the first point of call for key projects for Borsetshire Businesses.

If highly paid chief executives produce stuff like this, what right have we to criticise the younger members of our society?

A Typical Advertisement

Returning to letters written specifically in response to advertisements, we will start with an exercise. Look at this fictitious advertisement:

The World's Worst Letter?

On pages 112 and 113 you will find John Smith's letter of application. Please correct it, ignoring the numbers in the left-hand margin. You will be appalled and probably think it to be way over the top. Rest assured that I have received, over the course of the last fifteen years, letters containing between them all these solecisms and more.

At appendix 3 there is a detailed critique of John Smith's letter. The appendix is somewhat indigestible, but an hour working through it will repay dividends over the weeks of job-hunting which lie ahead.

'How did he manage to get one interview, let alone fifteen?' you may well ask.

A Suitable Letter

My original plan was not to produce an example of a good letter written in response to an advertisement, but I feel that you would, rightly, consider the omission to be a cop-out, so Peter Brown's response is on page 114. I would interview Brown, but not Smith. So, I suspect, would nine out of ten recruitment consultants or personnel directors. Why? Read Brown's letter and decide for yourself.

*   *   *

Why would I interview Brown? In short, his letter:
– States clearly what the job is and where the advertisement was seen.
– Emphasises the key characteristics which match the advertiser's requirements.
– Has sex appeal (karate and hand-guns).
– Removes logistic issues (location) from the decision-making process.
– Looks good.

a. **States clearly what the job is and where the advertisement was seen**

Many counsellors say that this is superfluous information if the reference number is given. I do not agree, for two reasons. First, because it is a convenient way of starting a letter (rather like 'How do you do?' when you shake someone's hand). Secondly, because we frequently advertise in more than one paper/magazine/journal, we wish to know where the candidate saw the advertisement. This is where so many outplacement counsellors give away their ignorance – but if they had waded through five hundred-odd replies to an advertisement in three different media they would understand.

b. **Emphasises the key characteristics which match the advertiser's requirements**

I admit I've made things easy for myself because Brown really does meet the spec. But does he? What I know, and you don't, is that he is outside the age bracket – he is, in fact, forty-seven. Many applicants in their letters draw attention to this sort of thing: 'Although I am outside the advertised age bracket ...' Why draw attention to this? I have already told you that I once got a job at the age of forty-five in response to an advertisement looking for people in the twenty-eight to thirty-five age bracket. Let us be quite clear: you should not tell untruths – but why point out the trivial way in which you do not meet the specification when you are the ideal candidate in so many other ways?

c. **Has sex appeal (karate and hand-guns)**

Frequently the recruiter has a lot of marginal decisions: do I interview A or B? In such balanced situations I tend to go for the candidate who sounds interesting – someone who will give a little zizzle to what could otherwise be a boring and unproductive day. Everyone has some unusual or interesting facet lurking in the background which leads me, if I am told about it, to think I'd like to ask him/her about that.

d. **Removes logistic issues (location) from the decision-making process**

Brown's letter certainly sets my mind at rest. There would be no hang-ups on the relocation issue. That's one concern off my list.

e. **Looks good**

You must be the judge of that.

The Value of the Glossary

Why was I nervous about giving an example of a letter which would get an interview? Because there is a danger that you will copy it and thus your letters will not represent your style and personality. Do, I beg you, write your own letters (note 'write' not 'generate'), but not from scratch every time. The concept of the glossary is well understood, I hope. For example, the first paragraph of Brown's letter is virtually a glossary paragraph – though the details must be changed for each advertisement. As you reply to more and more advertisements you will identify certain paragraphs which you use repeatedly. Put them in your glossary.

The secret of writing a glossary is not to write a glossary, for then it becomes stilted. Take genuine paragraphs from letters written in reply to actual advertisements and subsequently include them in your glossary.

Good luck with your letter-writing. You can be confident that your letters won't contain any of the horrors in Smith's letter.

My ref: JS/ADVT/5072/92/37B   Mr John Smith
                                   99 Waterfront Terrace
                                   Casterbridge
                                   Somerset

David McKintosh
96 Bonny Bray Square
Ochayblenoo
by Edinborough
EH99 1AZ

Dear Dave

I would like to apply for the advertised job in your company.

I believe that your main criterion is good line manager experience which I certainly have!

I have not got a CV but I can say that I meet your requirement completely, however I could generate a CV for your perusal if you need me.

I am looking for a job that will increase my salary and other benefits.

I need a high quality "executive" car this is very important to me for customer liason which I I consider is in my companies interest.

I do not consider that location is a problem.

I left my last job following a "policy disagreement"

34   at my directors insistence
35

36   I note that you require a degree or similar qualification
37   but I don't agree, I have met a lot of very stupid
38   people with degrees and I think you have got
39   the job description wrong and I am sure that I
40   can convince you that it is wrong which as so often
41   happens in recruitment by people who don't understand
42   the industry which is why I have had 15 interviews
43   but no final interviews but there is so much bias
44   against people without degrees don't you agree
45

46   I do not want to currently tell you my salary
47   as I was "grossly underpaid" for political reasons
48   and I cannot am not able to because I have been
49   in a great many jobs give you my salary
50   history because it was a long time ago but we can discuss
51   this criteria when we meet up.
52

53   I look forward to your reply in the very near
54   future so that I can meet with you?
55

56   Yours Faithfully
57

58   ⌁
59

60   (JOHN SMITH (MR)
61

62

63   PS I am soon going on a holiday for
64   3 weeks.
65

66

Tel: 071-998-2656   931 Orlando Avenue
                                                       London SW93 4QF

                                                       5th September 1993

David Mackintosh Esq
Mackintosh Enterprises
69 Bonny Brae Square
OCHAYETHENOO
BY EDINBURGH   EH99 7AZ

Dear Mr Mackintosh

                     DM/973:   CASINO MANAGER

Please accept this application for the above appointment, which was
advertised in The Times on Thursday 30th January 1993.

As you will see from my attached CV (annotated with salary history), I can
offer the following relevant qualifications and experience:

-    Honours degree in mathematics with statistics.

-    18 years' experience in the leisure industry in general and the
     casino industry in particular, with steady progress in
     increasingly responsible specialist and general management
     appointments.

-    Overseas service in Europe, USA and South America.

-    Fluency in French and Portuguese, as well as in English.

In addition, I have a black-belt in karate and am an expert shot with a hand-
gun. Both these capabilities have been of value on several occasions in my
career.

Relocation to the Isle of Wight will present no difficulty. Our children are
both married and we wish to leave London.

Yours sincerely

Peter Brown

Tailpiece

It is not only candidates for appointments who have a wonderful capacity for writing meaningless verbiage. This is the letter written by a chief executive in local government in response to an outplacement patient who wrote him a speculative letter:

> Thank you for your career history, which has only now come directly to my attention.
>
> From a reading of the brief, you appear to have several directions to explore – finance in the broad sense; management project work involving people skills; image and marketing projects; line management in a people-intensive industry.
>
> However, beyond this very broad targeting, I am unable to advise without at least a broad insight into the parameters of the remuneration package you are contemplating.
>
> Perhaps you can give some thought to this and then we can pursue the matter further, if you so wish.

What he meant to say was, of course: 'What salary are you seeking?'

To summarise:
* Decide what papers/journals you should see and establish sources, of which the library is likely to be the most useful.
* Reply to an advertisement within ten days – preferably less.
* If in doubt, apply.
* Carry out the instructions given in the advertisement.
* Emphasise the key characteristics which match the advertiser's requirements.
* Never make a letter longer than one page.
* Build up a glossary of good paragraphs from letters you have written.

12

Networking

*'There is only one thing in the world worse than being talked about,
and that is not being talked about.'*

OSCAR WILDE

The Importance of Networking

Why is networking so important?

You know that there are lies, damned lies and statistics. This particularly applies to statistics about how people obtain their jobs, not least because categories are defined differently by different people. For example, in the case of some published statistical studies it is clear that the category of networking includes speculative approaches. As we will see, the definition of networking is much more precise than that.

Nonetheless, there is enough evidence to suggest that a high proportion, perhaps as high as 60%, of patients handled by the big outplacement firms find jobs through networking. So the technique must become a major weapon in your armoury.

In recent years networking has achieved something of an unsavoury reputation because it has frequently been considered to be synonymous with pyramid selling. Certainly the mathematical concept is similar, but the underlying morals are quite different.

What is Networking?

What is networking as applied to job-hunting? Let me start with an illustration. In the mid-1980s my son Charles was in the Army in Germany and was thinking of leaving and moving into industry or commerce; so were many of his contemporaries. At that time I was Director, Human Resources of 3i Consultants. In this capacity I ran a substantial recruitment and HR consultancy and was also responsible for recruiting new consultants for 3i Consultants, including my own bit of it. I began to receive messages from Charles – phone calls, letters, etc. – the content of which could be summarised as follows: 'Hamish McHoots [Charles was in a Scottish regiment] is thinking of leaving the Army. He is a splendid fellow. He would like to be a recruitment consultant. I've told him you will see him in case you have a vacancy.'

Now this was deeply threatening. As it happened, I employed only people above forty, preferably nearer fifty. (This is because I believe that highpowered businessmen become somewhat fed up with being interviewed by so-called recruitment consultants barely out of school.) There was no way in which I was going to take on a twenty-seven-year-old chap, however good. Threatening, because I had to say 'No' to McHoots and, by inference, to my son. And, because we dislike saying 'No' to family and friends, we feel uneasy about it. A rift could easily have opened between my son and myself.

However, it was not difficult to solve that problem. I then began receiving letters which were couched in much more the right terms:

> Dear Mr Mackintosh
>
> Your son, Charles, suggested that I should write to you. I leave the Army in four months' time and am seeking advice about how to find employment.
>
> Please understand that I am not asking you for a job – Charles explained that you employ only older and wiser people. But he also told me that you were a tremendous expert in the job-hunting process, and in particular were full of excellent advice for those leaving the Services.
>
> So if you could possibly spare me twenty minutes and a cup of coffee, I really would be most grateful. If I may, I will telephone your secretary within a few days to learn if you would be kind enough to agree to a meeting.
>
> Yours sincerely
>
> Donald MacGregor

What did I do when this letter arrived? Yes – I picked up the phone, spoke to MacGregor and invited him to my office for a meeting and lunch so that I could give him as much help as possible in getting on with his future. The point, of course, is that we like helping people generally, and we particularly like helping people who are friends of our family or of our friends. This is the concept behind networking.

So what are the essential features of the successful approach? There are five:

1 A key
2 A comforting *raison d'être*
3 Absence of threat
4 Flattery
5 Action plan

I will return to these specific points after a more general explanation of the networking concept.

Cascading Mathematics

First, a brief mathematical diversion in which you can participate. Place your chessboard on the table in front of you and fetch that large jar of rice from the kitchen. Now put one grain of rice on the square at the left-hand end of the nearest row (square a1 in chess terms). Then put two grains on the next square to its right, four on the next square, and so on. By the time you reach the end of the nearest row, the eight squares will have on them 1, 2, 4, 8, 16, 32, 64, and 128 grains respectively. Now go up a row and carry on doubling-up.

This entertainment won't last long. You will run out of both space and rice very quickly. If you could continue, the number of grains on a square would exceed the world's human population before you were half-way across the board.

Incidentally, if you have ever considered doubling up on red at roulette, this experiment should disabuse you of that bright idea. Nevertheless, there is something of value here for you, the job-hunter.

Networking involves approaching suitable personal contacts with the aim of gaining access to *their* personal contacts, with the aim of gaining access to *their* personal contacts, with the aim ...

The cascade nature of this activity means that you can expand your list of likely contacts very rapidly. For example, if you start off with three contacts, and each of these gives you three more, and so on, the growth sequence is 3, 9, 27, 81, 243, 729 ... Of course, things will never happen exactly like that. Your initial list will probably be greater than three. Conversely, many contacts will provide less than three new contacts – perhaps even none. But the spread of contacts flowing out from your initial approaches will inexorably grow. (See diagram opposite.)

Note that this has nothing to do with applying direct to companies for a job. Nor is networking generally concerned with approaching recruitment professionals – unless they are personal friends, or contacts of friends, or contacts of contacts of friends. To a recruitment professional who is not a buddy you are merely a few thousand pounds on the hoof and he or she is certainly not going to pass you on to

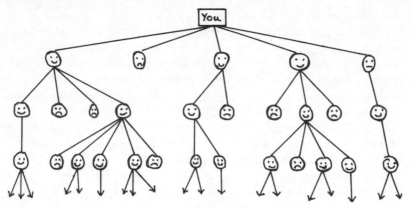

network contacts lest that fee remains unearned. Indeed, the best networkee (for the early approaches anyway) is someone who has no power to find you a job, because in that case there is no threat.

The Initial List

Draw up an initial list of possible contacts – four or five will do for starters – and write to them. I recommend writing rather than phoning, as a telephone chat can be misunderstood, whereas a letter can be very clear about what you are or are not asking for. The letter you write will have the structure already described, although as the addressee is your own personal contact the key is straightforward.

Many people have a mental blockage over the list of first-layer networking contacts, because they relate the whole thing to finding a job rather than to making lots of contacts which will successively lead them through the maze to the pot of gold at the centre. The ideal networkee is, I suggest, a businessman whom you encountered in your past who was a main board director of a substantial group and who has been retired for two or three years. Sure, he's got a couple of non-executive directorships, but he has no executive power, has no office to go to or secretary to organise his life, and is fed up with gardening and taking his wife shopping. He would love the excuse to talk to old friends and contacts. There really is no threat – as he cannot offer you a job. I can think of one case where the chap was so enthusiastic that he came up with eighteen names and remained a key player throughout the job search.

I also recall a discussion I had with one outplacement patient, Archie, during which we discussed this concept and came up with the brilliant idea that the ideal networkee should live in the USA! Archie had been in a job some years previously which had a strong transatlantic content. No threat problem here, particularly as his letter made it clear he wasn't seeking to emigrate to America. But the very fact that he had been dealing with these contacts on an industrial-hands-across-the-sea basis meant that they were the sort of people who were themselves into industrial-hands-across-the-sea business. And an introduction to a third party in the UK who wanted to continue friendly relations with his American customer (offset agreements and all that) meant a high probability of favourable reception from that third party at the next stage of the networking.

Of course, the idea of finding a job by somewhat devious means is not new. You may recall the Judge in *Trial by Jury*:

> *I soon got tired of third-class journeys*
> *And dinners of bread and water,*
> *So I fell in love with a rich attorney's*
> *Elderly, ugly daughter.*

Networking Letters

To return to the basic concept of networking as part of the job-hunt, let's assume that you now write to one of your primary contacts. In this case the opening letter is to James Baxter, a lawyer whom you occasionally meet at the golf club. Your letter might run like this:

> Dear James
>
> You are probably aware that there are big changes at Hamworth Industrials following the takeover by Blogworthy Holdings. International affairs are now being handled by the holding company, so all seventeen jobs in the International Strategic Marketing Department have gone, including mine.
>
> This letter has obviously not been written to seek a job – I am not a lawyer – but rather to ask if I might call on you for twenty minutes for a cup of coffee in order to pick your brains. On our occasional meetings I have always felt that you possessed both wisdom and a thorough understanding of industrial life in this area, and I could do with a little of both right now.
>
> If I may, I will phone your secretary shortly to see if you could fit in a brief meeting.
>
> I hope the putts are dropping.
>
> Yours sincerely

These first-layer networking letters will differ considerably depending on your style, the style of the recipient and the relationship. For example, with certain people my letter would be modified thus:

> '... if I might call on you for twenty minutes and a cup of coffee in order to pick your brains (you may feel twenty minutes excessive for this purpose, but I am in my sycophantic mode today). I have always ...'

The purpose of including this example is not to supply you with a letter to copy, but to give you the shape. You must write your own letters.

Assume you meet Baxter and he gives you three names. The first is Bill Normanside, the chairman of the local Chamber of Commerce and a very close friend of Baxter. This is a suitable network contact, since in his appointment as chairman of the Chamber of Commerce he is in no position to give you a job, yet he is likely to be a clubbable person with lots of contacts. Your letter to him will be similar in structure to your letter to James Baxter, but the key will be emphasised right at the beginning:

> Dear Mr Normanside
>
> James Baxter suggested that I should write to you.
>
> As you may be aware ...

The Essential Features

The 'key' is the name 'James Baxter', a close friend of Normanside, who probably receives fifty letters a week from people wanting various things from him. Most of these letters he may not even see. For example, when I was at 3i Consultants I got around a hundred letters a week from people wanting something from me. Unless the letter started with a name (the key), the staff produced standard replies over a photocopied signature. Thus I never saw many of the letters addressed to me nor the replies I was sending. The world of the word processor is truly with us. I should add that nowadays many recruitment organisations don't even reply to speculators. Expenditure on secretarial time, stationery and postage would be ruinous in these hard times.

But Normanside will be shown your letter; James Baxter's name will cause the secretary to put it in front of him. And he must do something about it, because, if he rejects you, he is rejecting his friend Baxter. So he probably won't bother to wait for your call, but will ask his secretary to phone you to arrange a meeting.

Let us now pause and go back to the letter you wrote to James Baxter and assess it against the five criteria listed earlier:

1 **A key.** I have just covered this.
2 **A comforting *raison d'être*.** People are nervous of becoming involved with job-hunters if they have an unpleasant aroma around them, so it is necessary to give the reason for seeking a job in the best possible light. By this I do *not* recommend the telling of lies, but it is always possible to put across the saddest of stories in a positive way. In any event, this is an essential part of the job-hunting process from the start and you will recall that you resolved this issue early on (see chapter 5).
3 **Absence of threat.** The first sentence of the second paragraph of your letter to Baxter covers this – you are obviously not asking for a job, so he does not feel threatened.
4 **Flattery.** Again, there for you to see in the same paragraph. People are so bad at flattery, but we all love to be told we are wonderful and to be thanked for our help.
5 **Action plan.** Very important. You must not leave it to the recipient to take action – if he does nothing you are fixed real good. Saying 'If I may, I will phone your secretary ...' is disingenuous as he is unlikely to phone you and say, 'Don't phone my secretary.' It sounds polite and not too pushy, but leaves the ball in your court.

Follow-up Letters

All this activity allows you to keep in touch with Baxter. Of course, after your initial meeting you drop him a brief note (I tend to use funny postcards with friends, but to each his own) saying something like:

> Many thanks for seeing me yesterday – I much appreciated the fact that I asked for twenty minutes and a cup of coffee and got two hours and lunch. I appreciate even more your thoughtful advice.
>
> I have been in touch with Messrs Normanside, Whiteley and Younger, and will let you know in due course what develops. But whether or not these approaches lead to gainful employment I am most grateful to you for your help.

Such a missive shows courtesy, but has a hidden aim. You hope that, when Baxter reads this, he will say to himself: decent letter, glad to help him; come to think of it, why didn't I introduce him to

Annabel Upjohn, who knows a lot about businesses relocating to the area? And he picks up the phone to call you to give you another lead.

So after the meetings you write Baxter another brief note:

> Just to let you know that I have had useful meetings with Bill Normanside and Sandy Whiteley (Younger is in Australia on business for the next six weeks). They both gave me some excellent ideas and useful contacts. I have also arranged to see Annabel Upjohn shortly. Your help in getting this far was without price and I am most grateful.

Again, you hope that this brief note will trigger another positive thought.

Your letters are beginning to reuse sentences and paragraphs you have employed before, so we are now building up a glossary. Let me repeat what I said earlier and emphasise that the secret of writing a glossary is not to write a glossary. That is, do not sit down and draft a glossary of useful paragraphs. They will probably read badly – forced and artificial. Rather, you should start by writing actual letters to actual people and then, when you are satisfied with a paragraph, slot it into the glossary.

It goes without saying, I hope, that your letters never exceed one side of the page.

Remember that no one ever reads a letter without looking at it first. *The first impression is all important; You never get a second chance to make a good first impression.* So, if your letter looks good, the recipient will approach its content in a positive frame of mind. If it looks cramped, untidy, scruffy and/or generally disorganised, you are on a loser from the start.

CV?

Should you enclose your CV with a networking letter? In my view you shouldn't, because CVs relate to job-hunting and therefore increase the potential for perceived threat. However, it probably helps the networkee to have sight of your CV before the meeting. So:

a. If you talk to him on the phone, offer to send it: 'Would you like to see my CV before we meet?'
b. If the arrangement is made through his secretary, you could send him a note confirming the appointment and adding: 'I enclose a copy of my CV, which you may find useful to glance at before our meeting' or, if he is a friend, 'I enclose a copy of my CV so you can see what sort of lies I am telling about myself these days.'

Better still, write to his secretary – if you were clever enough to catch her name on the phone – with confirmation of the meeting, and add the sentence: 'I enclose a copy of my CV in case Mr Normanside asks to see it before our meeting.' A secretary quite likes having letters addressed to her rather than to her boss, and will appreciate the trouble you have taken to get her name right. (As an aside, I would add that most executives work at about 70% effectiveness because they under-rate the contribution their secretaries can make.)

So much for the method of fixing those meetings. Now for meetings themselves.

The most important thing to understand is that the networkee (Normanside on this occasion) wants to help you. Not so much that he gives a damn about you, but, if he helps you, the contact who introduced you (James Baxter) will owe him a favour. Business (and social) intercourse is all about mutual back-scratching.

Network Meetings

If Normanside is a natural networker, he will know what to do. (Indeed, you should choose as your first level of contacts people who are natural networkers – people who carry a little black book and who collect business cards assiduously.) If not, you may have to nudge him in the right direction. In short, the key is to be receptive to his needs. If he wants to tell you funny stories, laugh at them. If he is obviously in a hurry, be clipped and precise. But your aim is clear, namely to acquire three or four good contacts to whom you may write mentioning his name.

The process of getting contacts must be handled with great care. You seek their names and addresses, and permission to approach them. The difficulty arises when Normanside says:

> You ought to talk to Mrs Gemma Robinson at the District Council. She is the expert on the expansion prospects of businesses in the area and works closely with the Chamber of Commerce. I'll phone her later this week.

You now have a problem in that you have lost control. A danger is that Normanside might not get round to phoning. A bigger danger is that he does, gets the message wrong, and calls you back in a few days saying:

> 'I spoke to Gemma Robinson. She is sorry, but she can't think of any useful ideas at the moment. She will get in touch if and when she does.

Consequently this particular networking channel is blocked, and there is little you can do about it but express your thanks for the effort.

So, if the offer is made to call on your behalf, indicate your gratitude and at the same time establish the fact that you would, in addition to his phone call, like to write. Doing this without causing offence is tricky and the method you select will depend largely on the mood of the meeting. There is, of course, another aim, but that must remain in your subconscious, lest you blow an opportunity through over-eagerness. That is to reach the moment when a contact says to you,

> As it happens we shall shortly be looking for a marketing director and your CV fits the spec very well. Hang on here — Fiona will give you a cup of coffee — while I have a word with the chairman.

Reverse Networking

There is one other aspect of networking worth considering — I call it reverse networking. It may be possible to identify some companies — say five or six — where you would quite like to work or, perhaps, where the top brass may have good contacts with people in your sector of the industry. (Perhaps you identified suitable targets at the trade show I suggested back in chapter 7). You could write to the top men, but you would probably receive a courteous 'nothing available'.

It is more effective to do some homework and produce a list of the key players in those companies. Then, towards the end of a networking meeting, if the atmosphere is friendly, you can say:

> This really has been most useful — I am very grateful. Incidentally, I have identified some companies in which I am interested, together with the key players. It's possible you know some of these — would you mind glancing at this list?

Don't then reach over and shove the list down his throat — this is enormously threatening. If you hold the list in your hand and advance it slightly, the odds are that he will lean forward and take it. By taking possession of it, the list becomes his 'property' — which means he wants it to be useful, so he will look at it with positive and constructive interest and care.

A Success Story

Does all this work? Well, let's take a specific success story. Earlier this year I had a letter from Brian Armitage, an ex-colleague. He had taken early retirement – one factor being that his wife was about to be ordained as a Methodist minister. They were to move to her new parish and he was looking for something in the area, having taken early retirement terms from his previous employer. His letter read, in part:

> I am writing to tell you that I have today accepted an appointment as … with … The importance of this appointment is that it was achieved through networking and had you not written to me your erudite paper on how it is done I would never have made contact with this firm and have been offered this position.
>
> This letter may be used as a testimonial without payment of royalties!
>
> Thank you for your interest in my future career and for your splendid advice delivered in your inimitable humorous manner.

I replied to him as follows:

> Many thanks for your letter of 22 May. I am delighted to hear that all has worked out to the good and I wish you all the best of good fortune in the future.
>
> Now to the *quid pro quo*. You have a choice:
>
> a. Arranging for your wife to invite me to preach on the third Sunday in every month from her pulpit. I will guarantee to speak for not less than sixty minutes on each occasion, probably reading the sermons of my grandfather, the great Dr H.R. Mackintosh (whom I may have mentioned from time to time), with footnotes provided by yours truly.
> b. In case this does not cause universal and ecstatic enthusiasm, I would settle instead for some quality introductions to firms that require services such as those I offer. I realise that Cheshire is somewhat distant from Oxfordshire, but I am sure that the quality of the client base to which you will have access will make such journeys well worth while.
>
> In the meantime I wish you and your wife the best of good fortune in your future life and would remind you that there is always a bed and a glass of lemonade for you here if you are down this way.

I reckoned that this was a pretty subtle way of drumming up more business and was therefore mildly concerned to receive the following reply:

> Dear David
>
> Thank you for your letter of 28th May with its messages of best wishes. Your offer of a choice as a *quid pro quo* for the networking idea is a risky step. After consultation with my wife I have arranged for you to preach on the third Sunday in September at ... Methodist Church. The text of your sermon will be 'Come unto me all ye who labour' which no doubt you will be able to turn into a marketing slogan for your consultancy service.

The only response was to send the following fax:

> Game, set and match to Armitage.

So that's networking in a nutshell. It won't necessarily get you your job, but it gives you something like a 60% chance. That doesn't mean that you can ignore the other 40%.

To summarise:
* Networking is an essential weapon in your armoury.
* The essential features of a networking letter are a key, a comforting *raison d'être*, absence of threat, flattery and an action plan.
* The best networkee may be the person least able to get you a job.
* Don't enclose the CV with your networking letter.
* Courtesy and gratitude may lead to further contacts.
* If you can identify a target company, consider reverse networking rather than a purely speculative approach.
* Don't force the pace — eventually a job will emerge through networking if you don't push it.

13

With Extreme Prejudice

'He had but one eye and popular prejudice runs in favour of two.'
MR SQUEERS

What Prejudice?

There is a great deal of nonsense talked about prejudice in the recruitment of staff. Employers of all varieties – public bodies, semi-public bodies, large companies, medium companies, small companies – desire only to find the best person for any particular job. No one would be foolish enough to reject the more able in favour of the less able if profits were to suffer, so forget about prejudice and get on with finding that job.

Nonsense, I hear you cry, and of course you are right. Our world is full of prejudice of all kinds, and it would be foolish to pretend otherwise. But my point is a serious one. If you become convinced that your failure to find a job is a result of prejudice, you will stop trying; it will not be worth making an effort, so why bother? So when you are rejected for a job, you should therefore perhaps appreciate the fact that the employer is looking for the most suitable person, and not assume that you have been rejected for some spurious reason.

Some time ago I read an article in a paper – one of those valuable pieces at the beginning of the classified appointments sections – about a woman who had found great difficulty in obtaining a job. From the first paragraph it was obvious she considered that it was all the fault of employers who were against her on the grounds of gender alone. Therefore there was nothing she could do about it, and therefore any real effort would be wasted. I hope what you have read so far in this book has given you the clear message that your future is in your hands; the worse things get, the more you must try. Easy to say, I know, but painfully true. Winston Churchill said, 'No one can guarantee success in war, only deserve it.' The same applies to job-hunting. There is no guarantee you will succeed if you do the right things with the right attitude, but your chances of getting that job will increase immeasurably if you do.

What Is, and Isn't, Prejudice?

What is prejudice? My dictionary defines it as: 'An opinion or emotional attitude (usually hostile) reached on inadequate evidence; unreasonable opinion'. The key word here is 'unreasonable'. We live in a real world and it would make little sense, for example, to appoint an Israeli as an arms salesman to the Arab gulf states or an Arab as an arms salesman to Israel.

We must also admit that we are all prejudiced. If I meet someone who claims to be without prejudice I know I have met a knave or a fool. We don't necessarily agree that what we have are prejudices — back to that word 'unreasonable' again. When I say I disapprove of caravanners who clutter up the roads and I would ban caravans except between midnight and 4 am, I consider I am being reasonable, in spite of the fact that thousands would disagree. It would, however, be ludicrously prejudicial not to take seriously a suitable candidate applying for the appointment of purchasing manager for a hotel chain simply because he spent his holidays towing a caravan.

What is or is not unreasonable is, I suppose, also a function of time. Thirty years ago it would probably have been thought unreasonable to specify that only non-smokers would be considered for an appointment; today most office jobs do ask for non-smokers, or at least those who don't smoke at work, and few would say that this was unreasonable.

The Hidden Agenda

Few people in the recruitment business would admit to the fact, but the employee specification for a recruitment assignment usually includes a hidden agenda. This is less so in large organisations, where the new employee is joining the whole organisation, than in a small company, where the relationship is bound to be more personal. As a recruitment consultant, it is essential for me to find out as much as possible about the client's prejudices before producing a short-list, which means attacking the subject at the briefing session.

Organising a short-list is like arranging a series of blind dates. What I hope for is that the client will, at the end of the short-list interviews, say: 'Well done, David, a really strong short-list. They could all do the job and I could be comfortable with any of the four candidates.' More probably he will say that all could do the job, but that he feels comfortable with two of them. If I have got my chemistry assessment wrong, the comfort figure may be zero.

There are inevitable personal prejudices which don't come under any specific category and which are hard to predict. Two (for men) are to avoid bow ties and beards unless you are being interviewed for jobs in a media-related industry or academia. I can't think why employers should be against bow ties; perhaps it is a perception of old-fogeyism or unnecessary flamboyance. And I do not suggest you should shave off your beard after many years nurturing it. I merely advise against growing one during your job-hunt; quite apart from anything else, you might look like Graham Gooch on a bad day.

There are, however, more universal prejudices, or potential prejudices. So let us examine the seven factors which may or may not lead to prejudicial treatment of candidates. I have listed them in reverse order of significance.

I must emphasise that, in general, these factors are on the whole most likely to come into play with jobs in smaller, rather than large, organisations.

Heightism

No, this is not trivial. On the whole it is easier for a 5' 5" woman or a 6' 1" man to find a job than if those two dimensions are reversed. This would rarely be part of an agreed hidden agenda, but I believe this prejudice generally exists.

An example. Some years ago I was invited, by the managing director of a smallish company, to find a finance director. The managing director — Ross Stephens — is an excellent fellow and a former colleague. He also happens to be 5' 5" tall. One very strong candidate was Dicky Dixon. The only apparent drawback was that he was 6' 5" tall. I phoned Ross when drawing up my short-list and asked if he might feel threatened by a finance director 12" taller than he was. He said, being a sensible chap, 'I am not sure. Possibly. Anyway, let's see.' When they met and shook hands, I felt that it was not going to work, and it didn't. Sitting down, chatting, they got on extremely well together, but those 12" killed the personal chemistry.

So what can you do about it? Not a lot, obviously, but, if there is great disparity of height when you meet your potential employer, you should sit down as soon as courtesy permits.

Weightism

In this case we are discussing overweightism. Here you can do something about it. If you are grossly overweight, you should take steps to slim down a little before embarking on a round of interviews. There is an additional bonus in doing so. Even if you were to get through the interviews, there would be a chance the offer would be subject to medical examination (perhaps a condition of the company pension scheme, for example) and it would be disastrous if you were to fall at that last hurdle.

Nationalism

Under this heading I am not referring to racism, which I put at the top of the list (i.e. the last), but rather a simple question of the country on your passport. Decisions as to what nationality would be acceptable or unacceptable are normally a question of practicability rather than prejudice. You might like to employ an American, but you cannot employ one without a status which permits him to work here.

If you seek a managing director for a newly established subsidiary in, say, France, you may prefer to employ someone who is French, not for reasons of prejudice, but because your business will probably make more money for the shareholders than if you looked elsewhere.

The development of the European Community has helped to break down practical barriers to employment within the countries concerned.

There is little you can do about nationalism when seeking employment; you either are or are not what the employer seeks. However, the reasons are likely to be practical rather than prejudicial, so we need not get steamed up.

Classism

It would be naive to deny that England is a class-ridden society. I deliberately say England, as this disease is far less prevalent in the rest of the UK. In 1912 Shaw wrote in *Pygmalion*: 'It is impossible for an Englishman to open his mouth without making some other Englishman despise him.' Is this still true over eighty years later?

The answer is yes, palpably yes, in much of our social life, but not, on the whole, in the employment scene. There are, I am sure, some areas where it is important to have been to the 'right' school, but I personally have encountered little snobbishness (in either direction) when employers are filling appointments. According to press reports, this is not so at two of our older universities, where there is an increasing reverse discrimination against candidates from public schools. However, that aspect of recruitment is outside the scope of this book.

One reason, I suspect, for a more civilised approach to classism is the increased number of women in work at all levels. My feeling is that women are far less inclined to judge people on their background rather than their merits than men are, perhaps because they have had to strive so hard to be recognised as equal members of the workforce.

I must admit here to an element of classism in my own recruitment attitudes. If, for example, I am looking for the managing director of an engineering company, I always look out for those who have started life as apprentices and worked their way up. Not only have they achieved a lot without any obvious early advantages, but they actually know what should and should not be happening on the shop floor.

In your job-hunt you should not worry about class. You will be assessed on your merits rather than on where you went to school or the length of your entry in Burke's *Landed Gentry*.

Sexism

Arguably the biggest improvement in this country over the last twenty years is in the reduction in sexist attitudes when employing people, but this change will take time to work through to middle and senior management in industry, although the process is well advanced in the public sector and also, to some extent, in the professions.

It is not really surprising that it's harder for a woman than for a man to gain a senior position in most companies, on grounds of experience alone. If one is looking for, say, a production manager for a company manufacturing furniture it is, because of the need for specific experience, unlikely that a woman has sufficient hours on the shop floor behind her.

And there are also personal considerations which cannot, if the EOC (Equal Opportunities Commission) will forgive me, be ignored. I recall the recruitment of a finance director for a substantial manufacturing company. There was no need for product experience. I might add that most employers always look for industry or product experience when making senior appointments. This may be valid when selecting sales or production people, but fresh thoughts from a different industry will often be a valuable and complementary addition to the team. A finance appointment is often a very suitable vehicle for introducing a fresh perspective.

The chairman (also chief executive) of the company was an excellent fellow with a distinctive work routine. During busy periods when he was discussing a particular issue with one of his directors, he was as likely as not to suggest at about 7 pm that they should go out to eat and return afterwards to continue the discussion. This later discussion frequently continued until the early hours. At budget time this might mean a string of very, very late nights with his finance director. During our discussion about the specification I argued strongly against appointing a woman. Not, I emphasise, that I questioned his probity or his wife's total and loving support, but the risk of damaging gossip was not worth taking.

The hidden agenda can also work in favour of women. In another instance the client company was a relatively new start up, the business being strongly related to sales and training. Both the entrepreneurs were male, aged roughly sixty and fifty respectively. We had recruited the sales manager in his forties. When it came to a training manager, we specifically looked for a younger woman to balance the team and to bring a different perspective to the business. A very high-quality field it was too.

Theoretically these secret agenda don't exist. Advertisements are, by law, gender neutral ('he or she will'), but I am sure that this makes no difference, a point I shall return to when discussing ageism.

There is one aspect of sexism which we must, however, take seriously. That is the rejection of a female candidate in a recruitment assignment solely on the grounds that she may require maternity leave or absence from work to look after her children. This raises some major issues and I do not want to embark on a lengthy diversion here. The purpose of this book is to help you get that job, and this subject is most likely to arise at interview. I shall therefore discuss in the next chapter the way to handle questions on the subject.

My impression is that a woman with children is not, on balance, disadvantaged in the recruitment race. The potential employer may foresee a risk of absence for family reasons, but offset against this is the perception that women who succeed in bringing up a family and building a career are somewhat special, from the viewpoint of both competence and determination.

So, apart from that specific point about maternity leave, I am not convinced that sexism is rife in the recruitment process. If it is, there is not much you can do about it as a job-hunter and it's best to forget about it, lest you start looking for excuses and do not do yourself justice.

On the other hand, I am sure that women do less well in the promotion stakes within an organisation. There is a tendency to see a bright lad with a future, but a secretary who is just a secretary. My impression, based on reasonable personal knowledge, is that America has a lot to teach us in this respect. However, that subject also is outside the scope of this book.

One final point on sexism. We in the UK are by no means the worst. A client of mine sent a field service engineer (FSE) to Madrid to sort out some problems with a computer. The duty FSE was, as it happens, female. The Spanish company refused to allow her to do the job, as it was perceived to be obvious to anyone that a woman would not be able to cope. The happy ending to the story is that a male FSE flew out to join her and they did the work together; the Spaniards were so impressed by Susan's expertise that they actually asked for her next time they had a problem.

Ageism

Ageism is currently the flavour of the month in recruitment. Much has been and still is being written about it. In front of me are many cuttings from papers and professional journals hammering the point: 'Jobless executives suffer from age prejudice', 'Discrimination against job-hunters over forty remains' 'The age of discrimination' 'Thousands of people in Britain are finding that few prospective employers will consider them if they are over forty-five and out of a job'.

There is a movement in favour of legislation to prohibit any mention of age in job advertisements (as is the case in the US). I am against this proposal. Age merely becomes an item on the hidden agenda. If, for example, there really are valid reasons to seek someone in the forty to forty-five age bracket, the omission from the advertisement of this part of the specification will merely lead to much wasted time and money spent on writing and sending letters which will get you nowhere.

Do not, however, feel excessively restricted by an age indicator. If you believe your skills and experience specifically fit you for the appointment, apply regardless. Perhaps the recruiter or the employer will, after the advertisement appeared, have thought about certain advantages of employing an older person.

What advantages? I think that there's a positive point you can put over. Let's say that a small chain of grocery shops seeks an operations director. You can point out that the appointment of a thirty-five-year-old could cause a major promotion block for all the keen, thrusting young store managers who would see their planned progress to the board thwarted, the brightest and best of whom might vote with their feet.

There is a strong case to be made for the appointment of a fifty-five-year-old (or whatever your age is around that figure). You would be able to tell the young hopefuls that your stay will be relatively short-lived, and that your prime task will be to develop their management skills to prepare them for that seat on the board when you leave. You, unlike a thirty-five-year-old, are no threat to their careers.

You will have to sell this idea to the managing director and also to all the filters — the recruitment professionals — barring your access to him. But it is a powerful argument and one you might, perhaps, develop during your networking meetings. Offer, if necessary, to come in on a fixed-term contract for, say, three years or less. Once you are in the job, you can make yourself indispensable. Your successful development of the aspiring managers will help the development of the business, so all your jobs will grow in scope. At worst, you should be able to clinch a non-executive directorship when you finish your contracted term. If you sell the idea properly, the potential employer will recognise the benefit in bringing your experience into the team without threatening the aspirations of others.

A similar approach is to enter as a temporary executive and make yourself indispensable. I discussed the question of temping in chapter 4.

That's what you do. What you don't do is omit your age from your CV. That merely serves to irritate.

Racism

We finally come to what is potentially the most serious and despicable form of prejudice — racism. Yet in the context of recruitment at executive, professional or graduate level, with which this book is primarily concerned, I think it is largely a non-event. That is not to say racism isn't rife in this country. Of course it is, but not, I think, in these scenarios.

Take industrial appointments. If I am looking for, say, a production director in a medium-sized manufacturing company, the specification probably calls for many years' relevant experience in a similar environment. It is highly probable that all the candidates who meet the specification have built up their careers over a long period of time in this country and in that specific industry, and therefore unlikely come from a racial minority. You may say — I am sure the CRE (Commission for Racial Equality) would — and you may be right, that the reason the members of the racial minorities have not been able to gain the right experience is the result of racial prejudice earlier in their careers.

But the shareholders of such a company cannot indulge in any chivalrous form of reverse discrimination just for the sake of doing so – it is essential to think of the health of the business and to find the most suitable person for that particular job.

In any event I am sure someone who applies for a job looks for excuses in the event of failure: 'I was too old/the wrong sex/racially excluded', when the simple fact is that there was someone better equipped to do that particular job.

This is not to decry the work done by those who have, over the years, fought racial prejudice. They have achieved a lot, but sometimes there is overkill. Indeed, there is a degree of backlash appearing – for example, a white employee of a county council made a successful case for a claim because he was apparently (and the tribunal clearly accepted this) discriminated against because he was white and not of an ethnic minority. In most appointments it is qualification and experience which count. When the playing-field is level, people will be appointed regardless of race. I would suggest that applies to the professions, such as doctors, lawyers and lecturers. Nor, I believe, is racial prejudice a major factor during the milk-round for graduates.

So my advice is to put the whole thing out of your mind and to press on with your job-hunt. Clearly you should approach the CRE if you have genuine cause for concern, but don't assume prejudice, rather than the fact that others match the specification more accurately, is the reason for lack of success for any application. If you do, you will become unnecessarily sensitive on the subject and this will become apparent to any interviewer.

To summarise:
* Do not excuse your lack of success in job-hunting on the grounds that you are suffering from prejudice. If you think negatively, you'll behave negatively.

14

Eyeball to Eyeball

'Boldly they rode and well,
Into the jaws of Death,
Into the mouth of Hell
Rode the six hundred.'
ALFRED, LORD TENNYSON

Interviews

You have by now replied to many, many advertisements. You have
networked assiduously. You have, perhaps, approached a few carefully
researched companies speculatively. And your work has borne fruit.
You have interviews in your diary – yes, not mere meetings, but actual
interviews with specific jobs in mind. You are now ready to ride into
the valley of Death, not with five hundred and ninety-nine companions
beside you, but alone.

No – you are not alone.

The Interviewer Wants You to Do Well

There is one important point to make about interviews which stands
out above everything else anyone can say on the subject. It is easy to
forget – particularly in a really testing interview – but you must keep it
in the forefront of your mind. I'll write it in capitals; if I could put it up
in lights I would do so: THE INTERVIEWER WANTS YOU TO DO WELL.

Well, it's obvious, isn't it? Take me. I've stuck an advertisement in
the paper and waded through six hundred replies, all of which have
had to be logged in accurately, many from people who can't, or can't
be bothered to, read: people who spell my name wrong, get the
address wrong, ignore requests that they should include details of
salary history or language skills or whatever. Out of the six hundred I
have picked about forty candidates, whom Pat or I have phoned. As a
result, I have arranged to interview twenty-five people.

Now I am sitting in an interview room in a provincial hotel or at the excellent Centre 3 in the Institute of Directors in London, with in front of me the papers of the six people I am going to see today. I hope every single one of those six candidates is going to ring all the bells. Six jackpots and I shall be a happy recruiter. I shall have the problem all recruiters yearn to have — how do I reduce six to a short-list of four? And I still have another nineteen candidates to see. Not only do I want as many as possible of my chosen candidates to do well, because it strengthens the short-list, but also simply because they *are* my chosen candidates. I have selected twenty-five people out of six hundred. If all twenty-five turn out to be unsuitable, my judgement is clearly at fault.

The worst day I can have is one when all the candidates I see are unsuitable for the job for which I am trying to produce a short-list and the client who is paying my fee. Thus, when I shake your hand in reception, before taking you through to the interview room, I hope that you are the one — just like anyone going on a blind date.

Remember this when you arrive at the rendezvous for the interview. It should help minimise the stress you feel.

You don't feel stressed before an interview? Very well, if you say so, but I wonder. Most of us do.

About ten years ago I was head-hunted for the job of managing director of a human resources consultancy. Naturally I was flattered, naturally I accepted the consultant's offer of a meeting and naturally I did some research beforehand. This revealed that the company was owned fifty-fifty by two shareholders who didn't get on; that there had been three other managing directors in the previous five years; that the published results showed a less than totally satisfactory trading position. Only a lunatic would have taken on the job unless it paid a very large salary contracted for at least three years, neither of which were included in the deal. Yet I went to the interview. Apart from the need to keep in touch with as much of the recruitment world as possible, it struck me that I might learn something to our advantage about the company's customer base.

I remember this very clearly. I was sitting comfortably in the head-hunter's reception area, reading the papers and drinking coffee. As I put the cup back in the saucer on the table beside me, I heard it rattle as I tried to put it down gently. OK, maybe I wasn't trembling with sheer terror; maybe I had a hangover or was wound up from spending forty minutes finding somewhere to park. But the fact is that I couldn't put that cup gently and silently down in the saucer. Not an earth-shattering event, but one I always remind myself of when getting out the rubber truncheon prior to interviewing a candidate.

As that candidate, you mustn't be depressed if the interview is particularly gruelling. Most recruiters would agree that it is the suitable candidates who must be tested. If I decide early on that the candidate is not the right person for that particular job in that particular company, I ease up and try to ensure a relaxed exchange of views. I may even put up with a fifty-minute story-of-my-life session – anything for a peaceful life. It is when I meet someone who looks progressively more and more suitable for the short-list that I have to probe the little nooks and crannies, as Dame Edna would put it, to minimise the risk of a disaster when he or she meets my client.

Preparation

So how do you prepare for an interview? First, you should do some research. How much you should do depends on the stage in the recruitment process at which this interview takes place.

At one extreme the research will be zero; this is when a recruitment consultant has placed a 'blind' advertisement, i.e. one in which the client company is not identified. Not much you can do about that. If the industry is identified in the advertisement, you may be able to glean something from a visit to your library's reference section, that same library which you found in the very early stages of your job-hunt and where you now receive a welcome because of your regular, friendly and well-disciplined visits.

In my view a recruitment consultant should not expect you to have done much research even if the advertisement identified the client company. A professional should be aware that job-hunting is a laborious full-time activity and there is insufficient time for a candidate to carry out a detailed search before every interview. But I fear that not all recruitment consultants would agree with this relaxed approach, so the message is you should do what you can, but you should not worry if you go to a first interview with a recruitment consultant knowing very little about his client company.

Things change, however, when you have an interview with someone at a company searching to fill a vacancy. If this is a first interview with the personnel department, you will be expected to have at least some basic knowledge.

The best source of information is the company itself. There is nothing wrong, and perhaps a good deal right, in asking for the last published annual report and/or sales material; you could do this when the details of the interview are being arranged over the telephone, or when you phone to confirm arrangements which have been sent through the post. The key is, as ever, to sound organised and pleasant rather than fussy or pushy. If you make the request in the right way, you will earn good marks before the interview.

When the interview is arranged, it is useful if you can find out how long it will last. People don't mind giving this information provided it is asked for in the right way.

Your Own PR Material

What about your own publicity material? You should take with you to all interviews the advertisement you answered, subsequent correspondence, spare copies of your CV and lists of referees and, also, photocopies of any certificates or other documents which help you to complete your story — for example a degree certificate, discharge papers from the armed forces, salesman of the year certificates, letters of commendation, etc. Although photocopies are not evidence in the legal sense, they are great comforters to the interviewer.

You can carry all this documentation in a briefcase, but there are some interviewers who don't approve of this method — perhaps they find a bulging briefcase intimidating, particularly if it is plonked on the table. Probably better is a zipped document case, which looks businesslike, but not too capacious.

Never, in any circumstances, thrust these documents at the interviewer. This is a very threatening gesture, and I sometimes find myself shrinking back into the protective comfort of my chair when I am attacked by bits of paper thrust at me like rapiers. It is much better for you to say, at the appropriate moment: '*I have a copy of the brochure I produced for that campaign here,*' gesturing towards your elegant document case, '*which you may care to see.*'

The interviewer will almost certainly say, '*Yes, thank you, may I see it?*' and lean forward to take the gently proffered item. And then a curious change takes place. The item now changes ownership. The interviewer has taken partial possession of it and wants it to be a useful adjunct to the conversation. The two of you now share the item, and this brings you closer together. As partners, you are now defending the integrity and value of the document against the rest of the world.

Dress

What do you wear? In the majority of cases a business suit, and this applies to men and women.

For men this is relatively easy, providing they avoid funny shoes or too outrageous a tie; I have already warned you against bow ties. In some cases (e.g. an agricultural foodstuffs sales manager in the extremities of the South-West) a tweedy country suit might be more suitable, but if in doubt, play it safe.

Women have a more difficult problem, in that they, collectively, have never fully accepted the unimaginative uniformity of the male approach to clothes and consequently personal decisions have to be made. The overall impression you wish to create is one of businesslike efficiency, so once again I would recommend conservative caution, eg avoid trousers.

So you are now prepared. You have done as much research as you deem appropriate, you have assembled a dossier in a smart leather document case, you look good. Conversely you feel slightly or very apprehensive, but you have the comfort of knowing that most of your fellow human beings would feel much the same in the same circumstances.

Smoking

Don't.

Actually there is an exception to this. If you are being interviewed by your potential employer and he is smoking, it is not a bad ploy to ask if you may also smoke. It forms a bond.

But, except in this specific instance, don't.

Punctuality

You should arrive at the place of interview about ten minutes before the appointed time − certainly not more than fifteen minutes and not less than five minutes. Being late for an interview is the eighth deadly sin.

It is no use complaining to yourself or your counsellor afterwards that you were fifteen minutes late because you could not find anywhere to park. You should have got there sooner and then waited in the car or some hostelry (lemonade only) so you could time your arrival with precision.

Very, very occasionally you may be late because of circumstances which are genuinely unexpected and totally outside your control, such as your tube train being stuck in the tunnel for forty-five minutes during a bomb scare or the Forth Bridge being closed by a major accident involving two petrol tankers. When that sort of thing happens, you should telephone to announce your probable lateness as soon as you can and apologise when you eventually arrive. I never cease to be amazed by candidates who turn up fifteen minutes late, thereby ruining my schedule, and never even hint an apology or an explanation. Their interviews tend not to be great successes.

When you arrive, be both businesslike and courteous with everyone you meet, starting with reception. There are some people around who are brusque or even downright rude with what they perceive to be the underlings, and then try to charm the interviewer. It doesn't work, because news of such behaviour is invariably passed onwards and upwards.

The Aim

So here you are, sitting in the waiting-room, as calmly as you can. Now your final piece of preparation. Focus on your aim – the ever present First Principle of War.

What is your aim? To get the job certainly, but that is too general. To go on to the next stage is better, but that doesn't focus on what you have to do now. The correct answer is: *to respond to the needs of the interviewer.*

No, I am not suggesting such an aim means sycophancy, but it does mean being sensitive. If, for example, the interviewer says, 'This is a preliminary meeting – shouldn't take much more than forty-five minutes,' then you are certainly not responding to those needs if you rabbit on, and on, and on well into the second hour. Or if the interviewer says, 'At this stage the name of the client company must remain confidential,' then any attempt by you to discover the client company's name will be futile and threatening. This may seem staggeringly obvious, but you would be amazed how often people ignore these simple points.

Now you are ready to ride into 'the jaws of Death'. What can you expect? An interview comprises a number of parts which can be likened to a three-act play with a prologue and an epilogue.

Instant Reaction

The prologue is the greeting stage. You have, I am sure, heard people say, 'I can judge a candidate in the first two minutes and I am never wrong.' If you haven't, I have. Nonsense, but they say it and believe it.

You would never be so foolish, would you? Actually, you do it all the time, at work, in the pub, at parties and when watching telly. No? I bet when you watch *Blind Date* you make instant judgements about the three candidates based on your first sight of them.

Not much you can do about it now. You have already helped yourself to cross this bridge by your preparation — research, dress, punctuality. Look cheerful, but not facetious, and look the interviewer in the eyes. And, above all at this stage, avoid gratuitous familiarity. Address your interviewer as Miss Jones or Mr Smith rather than Audrey or Peter. Then read the signs.

A helpful interviewer will address you formally so you know that such a mode of address is the order of the day or, if first names are to be used, will say something like, 'It's William, isn't it — please call me Audrey,' or, 'May I call you Elizabeth — I'm Peter, we're very informal here.'

If you are in any doubt, stick to formality until you are released from it.

Discussing the Job

Next will come the three acts of the play. The catch is that they are not conveniently signalled, as happens in the theatre, by the lowering of the curtain between acts. Indeed, in many an interview they merge into one, but you must have the structure in your mind, as it will help you to pick your way through it.

One act (normally the first) is the passage of information from the interviewer to you, telling you about the company and the job. In cases where confidentiality about these details is being maintained this act will be very short.

The easy situation for you is when the interviewer has something to tell you and wants you to listen. If this happens, do so: listen. If you are skilled at active listening, you can nod and grunt to show that you are listening without interrupting the flow. It is a bad mistake to interrupt; this is normally done to show off the extent of the candidate's prior research, but merely serves to irritate. The note you see the interviewer making at this stage is almost certainly 'Poor listener'.

It is much more difficult when the interviewer says, 'Well, what would you like to know about the job?' Of course, this gives you a chance to display some knowledge, but you are being invited to ask questions rather than make a speech. What you ask can only depend on the circumstances; perhaps, 'I've done some preparation, so I know a little about the company's history and its product. However, I understand that this is a new appointment, so perhaps you could tell me why it is being created.' (Yes, I realise this is not technically a question, but it will be read as such.)

Listen to what you are told during this act. Some interviewers like to feed you with information and test your listening capacity later. You will earn marks by saying, much later in response to a question you have been asked about some aspect of your experience, '... which you may feel is relevant in view of what you said about plans to build a new facility at the South Pole'.

Questions

The next act is when you are asked questions. I cannot tell you what all those questions will be. At appendix 4 I have listed some questions you might be asked, so you can think through the various ideas you might express. I have put it in this imprecise way because you should not prepare answers to a mass of specific questions – you must not be seen searching your memory for the answer to question 137, for then you will probably appear over-rehearsed and wooden.

There are, however, four specific questions which you may be asked at any interview and for which you must be prepared.

Tell Me about Yourself

Actually I ask this question only when giving patients practice in interview technique using closed-circuit television, and never when interviewing candidates. The danger is that a candidate will do just that, and do it interminably. I have seen a short-listed candidate take forty minutes to tell my client about himself – as a candidate he was dead after five minutes. But equally, undue brevity is to be avoided. Let me give you an example.

Harry Williams comes to see me for a speculative interview. I see him because he has networked me; life is too short to see pure speculators except those who have found a mutual contact. I start by saying, '*Mr Williams, thanks for coming along today. As I told you, we have nothing suitable on our books at the moment, but any friend of Bobby Robb must be of interest, so I thought we would have a brief meeting so I can put your details into the machine. I have read your CV with interest, but perhaps, to set the scene, you would like to tell me a little bit about yourself.*' Again, this isn't technically a question, but will be treated as such.

The first thing you must understand about this question is the

underlying statement I am making. Most questions are actually statements making a specific point. When, at contract bridge, a player asks
his partner, 'Why did you lead a spade at the third trick?' what he is
actually saying is, 'You really are a lousy partner. If you had any sense,
you would have led a trump as soon as you got in.'

In the case of my opening question to Mr Williams what I am really
saying is, 'I have got a note here to say that I am seeing you because
you wrote to me mentioning Bobby Robb. I glanced at your CV but
can't remember a damn thing about you. I'm tired and you are the
eighth person I have seen today and I have got a stack of phone calls
to make this evening. So please tell me who you are to get me off the
hook.'

You answer as follows, *'My name is Harry Williams. I am a
production manager and I am looking for a job because I have been made
redundant.'*

My patients often produce an answer like this the first time they are
asked the question. It won't do. The underlying statement – to the
interviewer – is: what a silly question – if you had read my CV you
wouldn't have asked it and I really can't be bothered to tell you
anything about me. At least, that's the way it comes over. The only
thing to be said for an answer like this is that it doesn't take forty
minutes.

So you must prepare an answer to this question; not word for word,
but the shape and rough content. Even if it is never asked in these
terms, it will help you to see the shape and purpose of your career and
make the interviewer feel comfortable, knowing who you are and
where you come from. Furthermore, if you do this well, you can to
some extent write the agenda for the interview. By this I mean that
you can 'flag' your answer, picking out bits of your experience or
knowledge which are relevant to the discussion in hand, leading the
interviewer towards those topics on which you are strongest. You
must understand that many interviewers – and this is particularly true
at short-list – are not professionals and are glad to respond to the
flags. If, for example, you were to say, '... It was during this time that
my team increased sales of air-conditioning units in Alaska by sevenfold
– which you may feel relevant to your aim to increase your sales of
central heating boilers in Tunisia ...' you can be pretty sure your
future employer (yes, you *will* get the job) will jot down 'Alaska' on
his pad and subsequently ask you how you did it.

Your answer to this question should take between ninety and one
hundred and twenty seconds; you can say a lot in that time. The basic
structure will be common regardless of the specific scenario, but your
flags will be selected to emphasise your achievements and strengths

particularly relevant to the appointment being discussed. You must, furthermore, round off your answer to show that you have finished talking. When I ask this question of patients, I note that I sometimes become embarrassed, and therefore feel threatened, when I suddenly realise that the speaker has finished talking and I have failed to respond. So a neatly drawn line at the end of that 90/120 seconds reassures me.

Much as I dislike giving specific examples (because they lead to standard CVs, letters, answers), I am now going to give an example of this sort of thing because the concept may well be unfamiliar to you. But please do understand that this is just one possible solution rather than the only right way of doing it.

To be of any value it is necessary to take a specific example, so this might be the reply given by Peter Brown, who wrote a letter applying for the job of Casino Manager on the Isle of Wight (see chapter 11).

> Well, Mr Mackintosh, I'd just like to thank you for seeing me this morning. I come from Yorkshire, where my father was – still is – a dentist. After grammar school I read maths at Inverness University, where I got a second.
>
> I started my career with Global Hotels as a management trainee working through all departments and in various parts of the world – mainly Europe and the Americas. During this time I found I had an aptitude for languages, which you mention in your advertisement and you may wish to come back to this point later.
>
> When Global Hotels established a casino chain, I was offered the job of Worldwide Marketing Manager, and enthusiastically accepted it. After three years in that job I was made Operations Director. For five years I opened casinos all over the world. In view of the start-up nature of the job under discussion you might like me to expand later on my experiences – though I hope that the Isle of Wight won't present as complex a problem as Baghdad.
>
> Some of the places I went to were pretty wild, so I learnt karate and how to shoot a pistol. Quite useful too – though I don't expect you want to hear my war stories today.
>
> As you are aware, Global has sold its casino chain. So I am looking for a job. Having rushed around the world for many years, I would quite like to grow some roots and also grow a new project – and I believe I could bring what you need to this job. My wife and I would like to leave London. Relocation to the Isle of Wight would be no problem – particularly as our children are married and away from home.
>
> That's a summary of Peter Brown to date. I hope it gives you enough to go on.

Something along these lines should open up an interesting discussion.

Some interviewers find this too short and too quick, but it is much better that one interviewer should want to hear more from you than that another – or most others – should be bored witless.

Why Are You Looking for a Job?

This is the second question which you must be prepared to answer. In the example given above I slipped it in to the answer to the 'Who are you?' question, but only because it was simple and quick. Normally you are better to leave it to a separate question.

We discussed the matter of what you should tell the world back in chapter 5. The rules I gave before apply just as much at interview:
- Tell the truth.
- Tell the story in a light favourable to you.
- Keep it short; the longer you go on the more fishy it sounds.

If you are currently in a good job you may be cross-examined closely as to why you are thinking of making a move. If the job you have applied for is obviously a step up your career ladder, you should have no difficulty in composing the answer. Similarly you may wish, for easily explained reasons, to relocate – and the job for which you have applied meets your geographical aspirations.

It is, however, possible to postulate a scenario where you cannot say very much in reply to the 'why move?' question. Suppose, for example, you are a woman being sexually harassed at work and you have decided it would be preferable to move away rather than to start a legal battle. (I am not, of course, saying you should not start that battle, but merely hypothesising in this example that you have decided to go job-hunting.) I am sure you can ward off any probing questioning at interview by mentioning the situation unspecifically and adding that the interviewer will understand why it would be improper to give any details. If you do this in the right manner, you will, I believe, gain credit for both your discretion and your wise judgement in deciding to move away from the problem.

You will appreciate that the 'Why are you looking for a job?' question should not arise if you are head-hunted. If you were to be asked, the answer is easy, *'I'm not really. I'm very happy where I am and I believe I'm making a useful contribution. But I was, naturally, both intrigued and flattered by your approach, and I'm here to see if it might be in the interests of both sides to take the matter further.'*

Why You?

By this I mean 'Why are you the right person for the job?' It is difficult
to offer much help here as the answer will depend on the actual job to
be filled and your skills and experience, and how you can match them.

The catch is that you don't know how the interviewer will approach
the subject. Some interviewers go straight at it: 'Why do you think
you are particularly suited for this appointment?' Personally I think it
is a pretty silly form of questioning, because a typical reply is likely to
be a tedious repetition of the advertisement: 'Because I am a dynamic
manager with excellent communications skills fully experienced in ...' I
would approach it from the angle 'What did you learn from your time
at ...?' and decide for myself whether the candidate is a dynamic
manager with excellent communication skills, etc.

If you have thought carefully about your answer to the 'Who are
you?' question, and targeted it at the appointment under discussion,
your preparation will be of inestimable value in answering the 'Why
you?' question, even if that first 'Who are you?' question is never
asked. This is why I said earlier that your work in preparing the answer
to the first question will help you through the interview.

Variations on a Theme

The interview will now develop in one of several ways. It may
comprise a question and answer session or may be more of a discussion.
You can only be yourself and respond to what you perceive to be the
interviewer's needs. It will help if you have thought about the answers
to the questions at appendix 4, but I re-emphasise that you should not
learn answers parrot-fashion. Merely use them as a vehicle for thinking
about being interviewed and considering the sort of direction your
answers might take.

Unanswerable Questions

You will probably know from your own experience that a really
dangerous person in any organisation is someone who pretends to
know the answer to a question, but who really doesn't, or someone
who says that something has been done when it hasn't. One way to
test for this sort of candidate, whose presence on the short-list is to be
avoided, is to ask an unanswerable question.

These fall into two categories. The first is a question based on fabrication. Let us say that about five years ago, in a different company, you worked on the launch of the JX 97 model (of what is not important). Having done my homework to ensure there is no such thing, I ask, 'Do you think that the TX 99 is an improvement on the JX 97?' You would, I am sure, be wise enough to say that you are not familiar with the TX 99. Some candidates, I regret to say, try to bluff me with a spurious answer.

The second type of unanswerable question has a genuine answer which is probably not known to the candidate: 'What was your company's return on assets compared with those of your main competitors in the last three financial years?' You may know the answer to this; in which case you had better be right. More likely you don't know the answer and your reply, 'I'm sorry, I don't know,' is a big plus on your side and separates you from the bluffers.

Invasion of Privacy?

We now come to the most difficult questions of all – personal questions which may or may not appear to you to be an invasion of privacy. I put it in this somewhat convoluted fashion because perception is what matters. I recently debriefed two candidates who had been interviewed by a client of mine – a client who likes to get to know candidates really well and who digs deep into all aspects of family and social background. He doesn't pry just for the sake of doing so, but rather because he believes that he needs all possible information in order to determine if there is a match between company and candidate. In view of the fact that this is a small, growing company this approach seems to me to be reasonable.

One of these candidates – they were both in their late twenties – found this line of questioning deeply threatening; the other was totally unconcerned. Incidentally, they both got a job in the company.

I mentioned that this was a small (fewer than fifty employees) company. This is, I suggest, a relevant factor. If you apply for a job in a substantial organisation, it should have both the personnel systems and flexibility to cope with all manner of personal problems, but, if you are looking for a job in a smaller company, other considerations may apply. Take maternity leave, for example. If the company is really small, say comprising three employees, all of whom work long hours, it may be destroyed if it has to pay for someone to replace one third of its workforce during a spell of maternity (or, indeed, paternity) leave. Which is why much employment legislation is concerned with organisations employing a minimum number of people.

So how does this affect you, the candidate, exposed to these questions which you may consider intrusive? I return to my basic premise about interviews. First, the interviewer wants you to do well and would probably not bother to pursue sensitive matters if there were no apparent fit between you and the job. Secondly, you cannot turn a job down until it has been offered to you. So answer the questions truthfully and in a friendly manner – a soft answer usually turns away wrath. If you feel threatened, keep your cool and do your best to deflect the question in a relaxed fashion. An interviewer tends to react against a candidate who becomes agitated, for agitation often indicates something to hide. You are a well-balanced sensible person with nothing to hide, so don't let those hackles rise.

After all, your potential employer may be testing you to see if you have the interpersonal skills to deal with his most difficult customer at the highest level.

Logistics

Just before the end – particularly with an interview with a personnel manager or consultant – you will probably discuss what I call logistics: rewards, location, availability.

Rewards

With regards to salary, there is a clear distinction between interviews following advertisements in which salaries are given, advertisements in which salaries are not given, and interviews during head-hunts.

If the salary is given, you should not have responded unless you were prepared to play the game by the published rules. (We discussed this in chapter 11.) If the advertisement said 'salary negotiable to £32K', you are wasting everyone's time if you won't work for less than £35K. Alternatively, 'Salary c. £32K' implies some room for negotiation, but not a lot, probably for reasons of relative salaries within the organisation.

If the advertisement does not mention salary, it is probably for reasons of internal security, in that other employees might react adversely if they knew how much the job paid. The interviewer may well be prepared to tell you confidentially what the planned salary is, but, if the process has been handled efficiently, this will have been cleared beforehand in the telephone interview to prevent people wasting their time.

If you have been head-hunted, there is more room for negotiation, but there will still probably be a ceiling in the interviewer's mind, which should be established clearly. Remember that in this instance you are being seduced, so a head-hunted interview is much more of a meeting than an interview of the style I have discussed so far in this chapter.

There are many people in the outplacement game who claim all interviews are, in fact, meetings of equals and that the candidate should control the structure as he thinks fit. This is lousy advice. If you take charge, you are effectively indicating that in your opinion the interviewer doesn't know how to do the job.

As far as other rewards are concerned, there is probably relatively little room for negotiation, since employers do not, understandably, like to upset company policy for a new employee. Take cars, for instance. If we are discussing a large company, there will probably be no room for manoeuvre because the company's policy will be written in tablets of stone. Indeed, I remember recruiting a manager for a £600M turn-over company; the assignment nearly failed after one (apparently) ideal candidate withdrew because neither side would give way on $\frac{1}{2}$-litre of engine capacity.

In smaller companies there may be more flexibility, particularly with a job at the top. However, since people who argue heatedly about their cars are seen as pains in the neck, my advice is don't make a fuss.

Location

One area where there may be room for negotiation, particularly in small companies when there is no defined policy, is in the reimbursement of expenses for relocation. A word of warning here: the situation on money paid for relocation can be delicate for reasons of tax. Normally it is best for the new employer to pay the bills (e.g. surveyors, lawyers, removal firms) direct rather than to the new employee. However, this is a matter for the accountant, who should know the current legislative position.

Which brings us conveniently back to this critical question of location. Making decisions on this subject was something you did early on as part of your first steps. You want to be prepared for this to be discussed at interviews and to relate your answer to the particular job. If, for example, you plan to commute without moving house, then do your homework. How far is it and how long will it take? Few employers are enthusiastic about people who spend four hours a day in a car; they will not be able to give their best to the job and the cost of replacing cars at frequent intervals is not welcome.

Availability

You should also think about your availability. Consider it under four headings: contractual, maximum, minimum and likely. If you are unemployed, you will probably be able to answer, 'Next Monday,' to all four. But, if you are in a job or in temporary employment, you must consider the implications. A typical answer from someone in work might be: 'Contractually three months; they might hold me to that; it is unlikely, but not impossible, that I would be asked to drop my car keys and leave; probably I would be available in six weeks'. With an answer like that we all know where we stand.

Subsequent Interviews and Short-lists

So far this chapter has considered primarily the first interview – with a personnel specialist or recruitment consultant – and a word about subsequent interviews is now appropriate.

What can you expect? Almost anything, is the answer. When it comes to employers – my clients – I have seen a wide variety, and all I can say is be flexible and sensitive to the needs of the interviewer.

It is not because these clients don't know their jobs, but rather that they have their own styles. Some like to start by talking at length about their companies and merely seek an intelligent listener at that stage, so active listening is the order of the day. Others go through the CV line by line. Some are interested in leisure activities, others not in the slightest. Some have a list of questions, others wait for candidates to take charge.

You are not, however, on your own. If you have been through the stage of a first interview with a recruitment professional (i.e. personnel manager or recruitment consultant), you have an ally on your side. Again, this should be obvious. In the chapter on Joining The Enemy I discussed the recruitment process from the recruiter's side of the fence. I told you how I would run a short-list to the client. At the end of the short-list interviews I want my client to push his chair back and say to me, 'David, a brilliant piece of work. All these candidates could do the job. Now we must decide which one gets it.'

The last thing I am going to do is coach you on how to get through a short-list interview with my client. That would be both dishonest and unwise. Dishonest obviously. Unwise because, if you as a candidate play a role that isn't really you just to get the job, it will end in disaster: you will lose your job, the client will lose his employee and I will lose my client. But if you are clever, you can still pick my brains –

remember, I want you to do well. So if you ask me, in a positive way, about whom you are to meet, what the programme is, the predicted length of each interview, whether there will be a tour of the company, etc., I am obviously going to be co-operative.

AOB

The fourth and last question for which you must be prepared comes under the heading of Any Other Business. I have already said that many interviews are lost in the first thirty seconds. A pity, as I explained, but the blind date syndrome is hard to counter.

Far more interviews are, however, lost in the last three minutes.

I refer to the response to the question which can be paraphrased, 'I've finished, have you?' The way you handle this question is a function of the type of interview. One thing you must never do is to put the interviewer under threat by insisting on an instant and publicly declared decision. For some incomprehensible reason various outplacement consultancies teach this as a sound tactic. They are wrong.

Let's start with the interview with a professional. The interviewer says to you, '*Well, thank you, I've got what I needed from our meeting. I much appreciate your coming along. Now, before I show you out, is there anything else you want to ask?*' As I have already explained, a question almost always covers an underlying statement. In this case the statement is: 'I've got what I need from the meeting and the next candidate is waiting. Would you please go away?'

Believe it or not, people are often taught by counsellors to respond thus: 'I feel I could do this job very well. Before I go I would like to be sure that you agree. Are there any areas about my application which worry you or about which you are doubtful, so that I can reassure you here and now?' or words to that effect.

This is deeply threatening and bloody rude. You are effectively saying, 'You call yourself a professional and say this meeting is over. Not as far as I'm concerned. Either say now that you'll short-list me or we'll go on until you do — because I don't think you've got enough information to reject me.' At this stage I murmur that I have enough to go on, remove you from the scene as fast as I can, and write 'NO' against your name on my interview list.

The correct answer, which you should be able to work out for yourself, is: '*No, thank you,*' rising to your feet so that I know you are going to move out and not waffle on, '*I am most grateful to you for a most enjoyable and interesting meeting, and I look forward to hearing your decision in due course*'. 10/10 and three gold stars.

A Quarterback Option Play

This becomes more difficult at short-list, because you don't know if the potential employer – say the managing director – actually wants you to ask questions or to go away. And even more difficult is an interview with the final arbiter – say the company's chairman.

Let us take a specific example. You applied for a job as production director of a furniture manufacturer turning over £30M. You survived the first interview with a recruitment consultant and were short-listed. Henry Blenkinsop, the managing director, saw you last week. The following evening he rang you and said, 'I would like you to join our company. There is, however, one final stage. That is, a meeting with our chairman, Sir Patrick Dodds. I've arranged this for 12 noon the day after tomorrow. Can you make it?'

You are delighted and agree. You offer to phone Sir Patrick's secretary and confirm. This you do. Having read this book carefully, you ask her, in a very unpressurising way, how long the meeting will take. She tells you that the chairman has a luncheon appointment at 12.45, so 'I expect about half an hour'.

You phone the consultant. She isn't much help as she hasn't met Sir Patrick, but she sounds very confident and says that Blenkinsop is very keen to appoint you, so the final meeting should be something of a formality.

You arrive at Sir Patrick's office at 11.50 and make friendly contact with his secretary, Claire Vickers. You confirm that there are no changes to Sir Patrick's diary.

The meeting goes well. Nothing substantial is discussed, but you feel comfortable with Sir Patrick and he appears to feel comfortable with you. At 12.25 he glances at his watch and says, '*Very glad to have met you, Mr Williams. Now is there anything else you would like to ask before I go off to lunch?*'

The trouble is that you don't really know what sort of person he is and what his underlying statement is. It may be 'Will you please go away. I'm happy and there's nothing more to say' (type A). If so, if you start rabbiting on with detailed and specific questions, you will upset him, first because he wants you to go away and secondly because he will feel threatened if the questions are so detailed and specific that he doesn't know the answers. Alternatively, he may be saying, 'This is a critical moment. I always judge people by the quality of the final questions they ask. I expect to hear something really interesting now' (type B). If this is the case, you won't do yourself much good if you leap to your feet and rush out of the door.

So you employ what is called in American football a quarterback option play. (This is when the quarterback decides whether to pass to a receiver or hand off to a running back — or even scramble himself — after, rather than before, the snap.) You give him an answer that satisfies both types: *'Just to say, Sir Patrick, thank you very much indeed for a most interesting meeting. Yes, I do have some questions, but I expect you would prefer for me to continue the discussion with Mr Blenkinsop.'*

If Sir Patrick is type A, he will agree, shake you warmly by the hand and, before he sets off to lunch, phone Blenkinsop and give his blessing to your appointment. If, on the other hand, he is type B, he will say 'No, we have a few minutes left. What would you like to know?' Now you can ask a question — not, please, 'What is the projected growth in added value per employee over the next five years?', but something important although less precise, such as 'Perhaps you would give me your views about the development of management skills in the company,' which can lead to an answer as precise or as general as Sir Patrick wishes.

The same tactics can be used at the end of any interview to leave those concerned with a general feeling of warmth and mutual good will. For example, at first interview or a short-list interview you could always use the option play thus: 'Thank you very much. Yes, I have a number of points, but I expect you would rather leave them to any subsequent meeting'. Note that the expression 'any subsequent meeting' does not make an assumption that you will go on to the next stage — which could get up the interviewer's nose. Equally, it doesn't sound negative.

What Next?

At the end of any interview you would like to know when you will hear further news. If you're lucky, the interviewer will say something like, 'As you will appreciate, I've still got some people to see, so I won't be able to let you know until next week — say no later than Friday the 18th.'

In some cases — particularly at first interview — the interviewer may say, 'I'm afraid I won't be able to let you know until Friday the 18th. But I plan to run a short-list on Monday the 28th or Tuesday the 29th. Could you, please, reserve those dates in your diary? You will, however, appreciate that I can't guarantee you a place on the short-list until I've seen everyone.' This is a good sign, so you whip out your diary and make a note.

Incredibly, some people come to interviews without a diary. When Oscar Wilde wrote, 'I never travel without my diary. One should always have something sensational to read in the train,' perhaps he was also thinking of arranging interviews.

The best possible outcome is when you are invited to the next meeting there and then.

If the interviewer does not act thus, by all means ask for an indication of the time-scale, but, as ever, don't be pushy. It may be that an inexperienced interviewer hasn't thought about the next stage in detail and too much pressure from you could cause embarrassment. And your aim is, remember, to respond to the needs of the interviewer rather than to cause embarrassment.

Expenses

Finally, in this chapter, a note about expenses. Efficient operators should offer to pay your expenses – rail fare, petrol (unless you have a fully expensed company car, in which case do not try it on) and a degree of subsistence for a long journey. If the organisation with which you are dealing does not offer, what should you do?

If it is a major expense – say a flight from Bristol to Edinburgh and back – clarify the rules in advance.

If it is a minor expense, do nothing if expenses are not offered. Then, when your participation in the recruitment is at an end – say you are rejected after second interview – in your pleasant letter to the intermediary (see chapter 16) add a note about your expenses. If you get the job, you can sort out the interview expenses with the recruiter after you have accepted the offer.

Eyeball-to-eyeball interviews are not the only hurdle you may be asked to cross, and I will deal with panel interviews and assessment centres in the next chapter.

To summarise:
* The interviewer wants you to do well.
* Prepare a brief life history with flags – it will help you give structure to your answers and may help you to set the agenda.
* Be punctual and friendly.
* Your aim is to respond to the needs of the interviewer; avoid preconceived ideas as to how the interview should go and do not try to take charge unless you feel that the interviewer wants you to do so.
* Practise answering questions, but don't learn scripted answers by heart.
* Use the quarterback option play so that you can be all things to all men and women.
* Don't insist on making the close a threatening affair – if the interviewer won't (cannot) give you an immediate answer, don't push it.

15

Trial by Jury

'Cannon to right of them
Cannon to left of them
Cannon in front of them
Volley'd and thunder'd'

ALFRED, LORD TENNYSON

Extending the Decision-making

The interviews we have discussed so far normally involve two people, you and the interviewer. In chapter 6 I raised the possibility that HF might ask his two NEDs to join him in the final decision-making in his search for a commercial director for SHL. I suppose we could call that a minipanel interview, but the dynamics and interaction in that situation are much like the normal one-to-one interview, in that HF will probably be using his NEDs to advise him rather than as part of a panel in the normal sense of the word.

However, there are many situations where the real decision-making is carried out by a group of people rather than by an individual. Then you, as the candidate, face cannon right, left and centre. Such processes are panel interviews and assessment centres. The latter may include the former.

Are One-to-One Interviews Valid?

There is a fairly powerful body of opinion which considers normal interviews are not a good way to select employees: 'Recruitment firms' methods have low validity' is a fairly typical headline to an article propounding this view. The question of what selection methods are or are not valid is one which creates more heat than light. I am seriously considering writing an article called 'Are any of the many and often conflicting views questioning the validity of one-to-one interviews in themselves valid?'

I would suggest that, hard as we might try, all prediction about human behaviour is pretty much a matter of guesswork, particularly when we are concerned with people interacting with each other. Thus, as a recruiter, I might be happy to short-list you for one job but not for another very similar one, not because you will be a different person but because the companies and their managers have different styles. The question is, 'How will this candidate fit in at SHL?' The characteristics of SHL and its managers, and particularly of HF, are just as important as the characteristics of the candidate.

So the scientific approach is largely inappropriate in medium-sized and private companies. Many will disagree, and it would be a fair criticism of my view to say that most of my experience over the last fifteen years has been in that type of company and my perspective is limited. Though I would add I am not against a scientific approach in all matters; my degree is in mathematics and physics, I am a chartered engineer and was, at one time, a specialist in nuclear annihilation. But I remain to be convinced of the value of such things as 'automated assessment'.

Large Organisations

However, when we come to large organisations, the situation changes. If we have a big enough sample, it is possible to make some attempt at defining precisely what we are looking for and to measure candidates against that yardstick. The classic example of this was the WOSB (War Office Selection Board) set up in the Second World War to select thousands of army officers out of hundreds of thousands of candidates. WOSB was the assessment centre to end all assessment centres – three days, a panel of assessors, massive throughput. (I quote the Army rather than the RN or the RAF because the numbers were so great the statistical data was that much more valid.)

Today we find these more highly structured methods principally in two areas. First in large companies. Typically we can take one of the big accountancy firms selecting large numbers of recruits on the university milk-round. The selectors (or assessors) are not concerned with answering the question, 'Could I work with this candidate?' but rather, 'Would this candidate fit in to our culture?' (As it happens, one critical aspect of answering the second question is the answer to the first.) This sort of recruitment is likely to involve a full-blooded assessment centre.

The other situation which involves collective decision-making is when public or institutional bodies are recruiting. For example, the IPE (the Institute of Patio Engineers) wishes to appoint a director general.

This is not an *en masse* recruitment (i.e. only one person is being appointed), but sufficient people must be involved in the decision-making process to give the membership body confidence. (And, dare I say, so that no individual carries the can if it goes wrong. No, that's probably unfair in most instances, but not in all.)

Other instances when the selection of individuals will probably be by panel are government and quasi-government bodies, academia, charities, partnerships; doubtless you have encountered some more.

Panel Interviews

So how do you handle a panel? With difficulty.

Perhaps a better answer is that you don't try to, at least not in the sense that you can handle an individual at an eyeball-to-eyeball interview. As I've explained, at an interview with an individual your aim is to respond to the interviewer's need. You should be able to determine whether it's a coats-off-shirtsleeves chat or a rapid-fire question affair. But with a panel there is no one mood to identify and to exploit to your advantage.

Some advisers say you should identify the key player – who may or may not be in the chair. Easier said than done, and not everyone present may have the same perception as to who is the key player.

What you can do is to discover, if possible, the seating plan and the names of who is sitting where. If you are to be introduced by an intermediary, e.g. the first interviewer who has short-listed you to the panel, you should be able to acquire this information before going in. Alternatively, the secretary of whoever is organising the meeting may be able to help.

You will find that one of your problems when you are in the room is making eye contact with everyone on the panel. This problem will be exacerbated if you are surrounded by the panel members rather than if you face them in line across a table. If you try to include everyone in every answer, you will quickly get Wimbledon neck and create the impression of extreme nervousness. So the best approach is probably to answer each panel member's question directly to the questioner whenever possible. Tend to keep answers short – everyone in the room will want to be seen to be making a contribution, so the percentage of time you spend talking may be less than in a one-to-one interview. If you feel that your answers are too short, you can always add, 'That's the short answer – I could expand on it if you so wish,' the response to which should give you a feel for whether you are saying too much or too little.

Assessment Centres

The assessment centre – the title describes an activity rather than a location – is normally used (as in the WOSB referred to above) to select several candidates rather than one individual for one specific job. There are some organisations which will assemble, say, eight people who are competing for only one job, but mercifully this type of sadism is rare. So, assuming that the assessment centre is designed to produce a number of successful candidates (as in the milk-round), your ploy must be to be seen as a supportive team member as well as an individual. You may, for example, bring into a discussion someone who is somewhat silent or who is unable to get a word in edgeways because of other, more pushy, members of the group. This always earns good marks with the assessors.

These assessors, in addition to observing group activities, carry out interviews, singly and/or in panels. Additionally there will be individual activities, possibly including psychometrics, in-tray exercises (where you have a stack of bumf to process and prioritise against the clock), presentations and role-playing sessions.

Remember that the basic attitude of the assessors is identical to the basic attitude of an individual interviewer, THEY WANT YOU TO DO WELL. Some of the assessors will be line managers who have been brought in for the day when they think they have better things to do (they are wrong in this perception, of course). They desperately want to fill as many vacancies as possible today, so that they don't have to come back next week.

All the factors are in your favour, therefore. The assessors want you to succeed. The sensible ones amongst your fellow candidates will want you to succeed if you show that you want them to succeed. The pushy candidates will find themselves marginalised. So enjoy it; assessment centres can be fun, and the more you enjoy the process, the better you'll do.

Get Hold of the Marker Pen

One specific piece of advice for the assessment centre. It will almost certainly include a group discussion in which you are collectively invited to reach a decision on some knotty problem. As a group you will be invited, either explicitly or implicitly, to select a chairman.

If you have studied Stephen Potter over the years, you will know not to push yourself forward for that role. Propose the appointment of some suitable member of the group, preferably one of those with whom you have established a mutually supportive alliance. And then offer (probably by standing up and grasping the marker pen) to keep the record on the ubiquitous and inevitable flip chart. Now you are the only person standing up – you have the power – but your behaviour is essentially supportive of the chairman and the group. Your influence will be great, but you will be seen as a team member. The assessors will mark you accordingly and you can be sure of one of those vacancies.

Of course, if you can so skilfully play the part of apparent subservience whilst actually wielding power, you are a Humphrey Appleby in the making and should probably become a senior civil servant immediately.

To summarise:
* When attending a panel interview, try to prepare a seating plan with names before you go in.
* Unless the panel is small and within your cone of vision, concentrate on one questioner at a time.
* Allow members of the panel to talk if they want to; don't monopolise.
* Don't try to compete with your fellow candidates at an assessment centre; be mutually supportive.
* The assessors want you to do well.
* Take control of the marker pen and the flip chart.

16

Handling Those Offers ... and Those Rejections

'Never do to-day what you can put off till to-morrow.'

PUNCH

Rejections Are Inevitable

This is going to be an upbeat chapter, in which we are going to discuss how to handle all those fabulous offers that flood in. But before we do that, it is appropriate to give some thought to how you deal with rejections.

Advertised Jobs – Rejection During Screening

Take the easiest example first. You respond to an advertisement and receive, after about three weeks, a polite letter explaining that the response has been substantial, there are other candidates who fit the specification more accurately and therefore your application will not be considered further on this occasion. What should you do?

Ninety-eight times out of one hundred you should do absolutely nothing. Any action will be a waste of time (yours) and money (yours). You must assume that the advertiser received six hundred replies, selected twenty applicants for interview and sent reject letters to five hundred and eighty. If you write back asking to be reconsidered, you are effectively saying that the advertiser doesn't know his or her job. You won't do yourself any harm by your action (apart from the aforementioned time and money), because your letter will go straight into the bin, but you won't do yourself any good.

I am sure you are saying all this sounds arrogant and unhelpful, but you must remember that every letter which a personnel department or a recruitment consultant sends out costs money. If all the five hundred and eighty rejected candidates wrote to complain and replies were sent, costs would quickly rise.

What about the two in one hundred times that you might take action? If the response to the advertisement went to the actual employer who subsequently rejected you, it probably won't do any harm to write a very short letter expressing 'thanks for an early response ... disappointment ... very interested in the company ... if any further opportunities occur would be most interested ... best wishes'. It is faintly possible the recipient of this letter has just spent six hours interviewing four unsuitable candidates and might decide to interview you.

Flannel

When you write, make your letter brief and positive. Above all, avoid flannel.

The day I was drafting this chapter I received a letter from someone who had been rejected for a managing director's appointment at screening; he didn't meet the specification. Before I quote the penultimate paragraph of his letter, I should point out that I am a self-employed sole trader. I am not constantly filling the quality press with job advertisements. Nor am I constantly working for the industry in question. And I do not have an office in London.

> As your company has an excellent reputation in the industry
> and function areas in which I have an interest, an opportunity
> to meet with you on one of my regular visits to the London
> area would be much appreciated.

That is flannel.

One thing you must do with all these rejections is to add them to the score. We spoke earlier in chapter 11 about the idea that every rejection takes you one step nearer an interview, on the theory that if your hit rate is three in a hundred applications, then every time you clock up thirty-three more rejections, you should gain one more interview.

Refusals to Meet

The other type of early refusal you may receive is a network contact declining a meeting. Here you can do nothing directly. Next time you talk to the person who gave you that contact you may pass on the information – in a low key and non-whingeing way – that Mr X or

Miss Y couldn't help, but you must do that in the mode of providing useful feedback rather than of complaining.

Rejection After First Interview

When you have been interviewed and subsequently rejected, your next course of action needs some thought. It all depends on circumstances.

Take the typical example of an interview with a member of a personnel department. Let's say that Miss Matthews, a personnel manager in a substantial company, told you that she was going to interview twenty people and present a short-list of three to the line manager. There is not much point writing to say that she has got it wrong and you should be on the short-list. But in this case a brief friendly letter, thanking her for her time and asking to be considered for any similar posts in the organisation, can do no harm.

In this sort of follow-up letter you must not ask for feedback and advice. Some books on job-hunting recommend that you should do so. Why? Miss Matthews is not in business to give free consultancy. It is a threatening question anyway; she is unlikely to say, 'Because I didn't like the way you picked your nose when talking to me.' Nor, because she is a professional and has read all the books and identified all the pitfalls, is she likely to say that your experience in a certain area is a bit weak, as she knows you will (if you've read all those books as well) then bombard her with letters explaining that your experience is more complete and more relevant than she thinks.

Similar considerations apply if the first interview was by a recruitment consultant.

Rejection After Short-list

Let me remind you that a short-list may come about in one of two very different ways. First, it is the end product of the screening/first interview process and will probably comprise three or four candidates who will be presented, by the personnel intermediary, to the end-user employer. In this case you have already impressed the initial interviewer sufficiently to be included in that short-list.

Alternatively, the expression 'short-list' may be used to describe all those who are selected for interview. In this instance the screening process is a fine filter which leads to a list of, perhaps, four to eight candidates for interview with the end-user, ie without any personnel intermediary carrying out first interviews. This type of short-list often applies to public bodies, academia and so on, outside the commercial/

industrial sector. In this case you did, at least, meet the end-user employer prior to that rejection.

So the question is, should you write following rejection, and to whom?

A Success Story

My views about this have modified over the years. One case where a follow-up letter worked springs to mind — a transatlantic story, I grant you. My daughter Elissa, who lives in Florida, had to go job-hunting when the head office of the bank for which she worked moved elsewhere. She applied for an extremely interesting sounding job and was pipped at the post. She wrote to Michelle Meadows, who would have been her boss, saying '... disappointed ... super people ... would love to work for the organisation ... most interested if anything else comes up'.

As it happened, the person who actually got the job didn't settle in. The management committee discussed it and Michelle suggested going back to Elissa. 'Oh, no, we can't go back to someone we've turned down,' was the view — a view I admit to having expressed (wrongly I now think) on occasions to clients here in the UK. 'But', said Michelle, 'she wrote such a charming letter. I am sure she wouldn't be offended.' The result was that Elissa got an excellent job in a super organisation. Maybe it is possible to make one's own luck.

Since then I have seen some of my outplacement patients employ these tactics with success. The most promising instance is probably when the initial interviewer who short-listed you belongs to a large company or a substantial recruitment consultancy. Not so much because the same job may come up again, as in the case quoted above, but because there is likely to be a large enough throughput of recruitment assignments to make it worth your while being on the books. (One-man-band recruiters are unlikely to have another similar appointment to fill in the desired time-scale.)

Therefore I suggest that anyone who has short-listed you for a job should be on your list of contacts with whom you keep in touch from time to time. If, for example, you take a temporary contract, you should keep these contacts informed of the fact, giving your new availability. Provided you do it in a businesslike, brief and non-fuss-budgety way you will add to your collection of gold stars.

Success – an Offer at Last

So much for rejections, but what about success? All your work has
borne fruit and offers are rolling in.

You will recall that early in this book I said your aim was to receive
a number of simultaneous offers so that you could decide which one to
accept. Unfortunately life isn't like that. A much more likely scenario is
that you receive an offer and have several other possibilities in the
pipeline, some of which are well advanced and some of which are in
the early stages. How do you play the hand?

The Perfect Job

If you have been offered the perfect job, you have no problems. You
accept. By 'perfect' I mean everything is right: responsibilities,
prospects, rewards, location and, above all, a comfortable feeling that it
is the right job for you in the right organisation at the right time
working with the right people.

If it is nearly, but not quite, the perfect job – say the salary is a bit
low – you may have to do a little gentle negotiating. The key here is
to be really enthusiastic while you negotiate. If you are lucky in having
a helpful buffer between you and your potential employer, such as a
personnel manager or a recruitment consultant, the negotiation will be
that much easier. Both these intermediaries are hoping for a successful
conclusion and will work hard to produce a satisfactory outcome. This
will usually mean ensuring an element of WIN-WIN in the result of
the negotiation.

A Poor Job

Much more difficult is when you receive an offer of a poor job. Your
campaign has gone on for some months and you are growing desperate.
Any job, you feel, is better than none. Should you make the best of a
bad job and accept?

Obviously your decision will depend on the precise circumstances.
The accepted wisdom preached for many years by the outplacement
world has been that you should not sell yourself cheap or accept
unacceptable (to you) working conditions merely to find work. In the
recent recessionary years this philosophy has been modified as the
realisation grows that jobs are becoming harder to find.

Remember also that salary negotiation may not be a simple question of convincing the employer you are worth more than he is offering. There can be no measure (except, I suppose, in the case of a commission only salesman) of what somebody is worth in a job. The major issue is relativity with regards to those at a higher level in the hierarchy and those at a lower level, so do not necessarily think you are being done down if the potential employer says, '... Yes, certainly I would like to pay you more, but I'm afraid doing so would drive a coach and horses through my salary structure.'

There is one specific type of job I must warn you to be on your guard against. I call this either the 'knight-in-shining-armour appointment' or the 'magic-wand solution'. By this I mean a job created to solve a problem which has deep roots and which cannot be solved simply by appointing a new executive.

If, for example, there is a basic flaw in the design of a product and it constantly breaks down, the appointment of a new sales director is unlikely to make much difference. Or, if a leisure firm builds an hotel on the slopes of a volcano, it is not much good appointing a new manager if business declines dramatically when the volcano goes active.

You should also consider whether the style of the company suits *your* personal style. If not, it would be good for neither you nor the company if you were to join. I have in mind a specific example of this where I, as the recruiter, got it wrong. The style of my client company was of the late start/late finish variety, in that employees often arrived after 9 am, but could normally be found still working late into the evening. The successful candidate preferred to be at his desk by 7.30 am and liked to get home in time to play with his children. Nothing wrong with either style, but they were incompatible. Fortunately his previous employer was delighted to take him back after a few months, but it was a hicccup for both sides which could have been avoided.

So if you like to take work home to do after you have seen the children or tended to aged relatives, you should ensure your lifestyle is in tune with that of your prospective employer.

Take another common example. You might find yourself joining a company where everyone smokes heavily in the office. If this is going to upset you, don't accept the offer of a job with that company.

These are obvious examples. The reality is normally less obvious and more complex. I merely advise you to be careful about getting yourself into an appointment which is doomed before you start work.

The Delaying Game

Assuming the job is not obviously totally wrong for you, a major factor in your considerations will be whether you have anything better looming up. If that something better is reasonably close, you must embark on delaying tactics, with the aim of keeping yourself available for the two birds in the bush without letting go of the bird in your hand. You therefore bring your delaying tactics into play. It should, I reckon, be possible to buy three weeks without losing the job – but don't sue me if you get it wrong.

For example, let's assume the company has said that they will put an offer in the post 'today'. The letter arrives next day. Wait three days and phone and express concern that you have not yet received an offer. This will probably lead to apologies and assurances that another copy will be put in the post. Sound pleased and say you are looking forward to receiving it, but point out you will be away for a few days. You must then ensure that you personally do not answer the phone during the relevant period. When the second letter arrives, get your spouse or someone else to phone, saying both offers arrived in the same post, you are expected back on some day about a week ahead and will deal with the matter immediately on your return.

Give it that week and write provisionally accepting the offer, but asking a couple of esoteric questions. Not, please, about trivial topics which will merely cause hackles to rise, but rather about complex matters – pension transferability is a good instance. Reinforce your enthusiasm by discussing the start date.

Meanwhile you must put some very gentle pressure on those involved in the other jobs which are nearly landed in order to obtain an early decision.

Your 'opponent' in this chess game may be aware of what you are up to, but by now wants you to join and will not be keen to withdraw the offer – particularly as it is quite possible your position is totally as described and a late withdrawal of an offer could lead to trouble. The worst thing that can happen – unless you have been blatantly foolish in your machinations – is you will be given a deadline for acceptance, but by then you should have a clearer idea about other prospects.

The Ultimate Question

Finally, we come to the question you may wish to ask, but which I won't answer – in print, that is. Assume that you accept on 1 October a job with a joining date four weeks ahead – say 1 November.

Everything is lined up for your commencement. Then on 15 October you are offered a far better job at far better money with less domestic upset. What do you do?

In making your decision, you should consider the following factors:

– Your prime responsibility, at this stage in your life, is to your family and yourself.

– Companies rarely sue because a candidate withdraws after acceptance. (There was, however, a case in which a local authority did go to law because of the time and money spent on an aborted recruitment, so there are no guarantees.)

This may all sound very cynical, but we live in a hard world and employing organisations have been known to look after themselves a little too enthusiastically. There was, for example, an instance reported in which a City institution went on the graduate milk-round and offered jobs to all the best candidates, thus depriving the opposition of their services. It then dumped those it did not need before they had started work. Ouch! So my advice is that you must consider each instance on its own merits, but that you must look after the interests of your family and yourself. However, most employers are reasonable human beings, and you will probably find honesty is the best policy. If you are a professional person (e.g. an accountant or a lawyer), you must be particularly careful to handle the situation sensitively.

To summarise:
* At whatever stage you are rejected, do not make a fuss – it will get you nowhere.
* Do not ask recruitment professionals for free consultancy.
* A friendly and positive note to anyone who has supported you in the recruitment process may prove worthwhile.
* Do not necessarily take the first job offered, but do remember that we live in hard times and you may have to take a step backwards.
* If you have a partly satisfactory offer in the bag and better ones on the horizon, you can buy three weeks by sophisticated delaying tactics.
* Your main loyalty is to your family and yourself.

17

As the Sun Sinks Slowly in the West

'This is not the end. It is not the beginning of the end. But it is, perhaps, the end of the beginning.'

WINSTON CHURCHILL

Still Work to Do

Your search for a good job has succeeded. You duly start work. Now you can consign your files – this book, indeed – to the cupboard under the stairs.

Not quite yet. It is astonishing how often people fail to capitalise on all the work they have done. There are now three things I want you to do.

Relax

Do the things I told you not to do at the beginning of your job search – e.g. paint the garden fence. Above all, take a holiday.

Stand Down Your Network

You must tell everyone who has helped you that you've started a new job and are no longer on the market. Doing so is simple courtesy.

There is also an element of self-interest, because you cannot predict how things are going to work out. Perhaps you have been recruited into an ailing company in the aforementioned knight-in-shining-armour-galloping-to-the-rescue mode. For whatever the reason, you may find yourself on the market again. Your previous contacts (counsellor, networkees, personnel managers, recruiters and so on who have helped you in a kindly and supportive way), whose help you may require again, are going to be more than somewhat miffed if you didn't have the decency to tell them when you came off the market. So look upon your network not as something you have built, used and can now discard, but rather as the foundation of the network you will maintain for the rest of your working life.

How do you tell everyone? Yes, you've guessed it: by letter. If your new employer has an operation which needs general publicity, you can put out your closing-down-the-network letter on company paper and through the company franking machine as a PR exercise. If that condition does not apply, you must do it yourself. But one way or another, do it you must.

Review Your Life

This is also the moment for you to review your life. If you were effectively fired from your last job, you should consider to what extent you were to blame and how you might modify your future behaviour and actions. You don't want to lose your new job for the same reasons.

Even if you were genuinely a victim of redundancy, you might benefit from a little self-analysis. This is an appropriate moment to consult your counsellor for the last time. If this review leads to any need for change, make that change.

Valete

Now it only remains for me to wish you all the best of good fortune in your new job. You have achieved success through your own efforts and you can feel justly pleased. Thank you for letting me share the experience with you.

To summarise:
* Take a holiday.
* Stand down your network for this operation, but don't close it down. Use it as the basis for your future network.
* Review your past so that you can, if necessary, modify your future behaviour.

Appendix 1

Where to Get Help

This appendix is in two sections:

Section A is taken from the booklet published by BBC Education referred to in chapter 3. It is a comprehensive list and I reproduce it here (with repeated thanks). Not all the details are necessarily appropriate to you, since the very fact the list is comprehensive means that it includes some organisations whose primary purpose is to help those involved in confrontation. In this book I have preached the avoidance of confrontation whenever possible, in favour of WIN-WIN negotiation. None the less, it is rare to find such a useful list, so I include it *in toto* without pruning.

Section B lists some additional details which may be useful to my target readership.

Although the information is, to the best of my knowledge, accurate at the time of going to press, changes do occur and you may have to update it. The responsibility for any errors is mine and not the BBC's. Equally, neither I nor my publisher can take responsibility for the advice offered by any of the organisations or institutions listed below.

Section A

Citizens Advice Bureau

There's a CAB in most towns. They give free, independent, confidential advice and information on just about anything, including employment rights. Look in the phone book or, if you have difficulty finding them, call their head office: 071–833 2181.

ACAS (Advisory, Conciliation and Arbitration Service)

27 Wilton Street
London SW1X 7AZ
071–388 5100

This provides free help and advice to employers and employees on employment matters.

Birmingham Settlement

318 Summer Lane
Birmingham B19 3R
Money advice: 021–359 3562
National Debtline: 021–359 8501

They run a National Telephone Debtline to give advice to people in debt.

British Association for Counselling

1 Regent Place
Rugby
Warwickshire CV21 2PJ
0788–578328

Business in the Community

227A City Road
London EC1V 1LX
071–253 3716

CADE (Campaign Against Discrimination in Employment)

395 Burlow Road
Altrincham
Cheshire WA14 5HW
061–941 2902

For advice if you feel that you've been discriminated against on the grounds of age.

Career Development Loans
Freephone: 0800 585505

The Careers Service
Look in the phone book or contact head office:
3 Alfred Place
London WC1E 7EB
071–631 0077

Offers free career guidance.

Child Poverty Action Group
1–5 Bath Street
London EC1V 9PY
071–253 3406

They publish books on benefits.

Commission for Racial Equality
Elliot House
10–12 Allington Street
London SW1E 5EH
071–828 7022

For advice if you feel that you've been discriminated against on the
grounds of race.

Educational Guidance Services for Adults
National Education Guidance Initiative
c/o YHAFHE
Dewsbury Business & Media Centre
13 Wellington Road East
Dewsbury WF13 1XG

Information also in:

UK Directory of Educational Guidance Services for Adults
(published by UDACE)

Most towns have a service which provides impartial advice and
guidance on education and training to anyone who needs it.

Employment Departments
Look in the phone book under Employment Services, or ask your local
Job Centre or CAB.

Equal Opportunities Commission
Overseas House
Quay Street
Manchester M3 3HN
061–833 9244

For advice if you feel that you've been discriminated against on the
grounds of race or sex.

Fair Employment Commission
Andras House
609 Great Victoria Street
Belfast BT2 7BB
0232 240020

In Northern Ireland – for advice if you feel that you've been
discriminated against for political or religious reasons.

FIMBRA
Hertsmere House
Hertsmere Road
London E14 4AB
071–538 8860

The regulatory body for Independent Financial Advisers. They'll be
able to give you contacts in your area.

Free Representation Unit
13 Gray's Inn Square
London WC1R 5JP
071–831 0692

Provides free representation to people who can't afford to pay for
representation at industrial tribunals.

The Industrial Society
Robert Hyde House
48 Bryanston Square
London W1H 7LN
071–262 2401

Can advise member firms on handling redundancies and other employment matters.

IPM (Institute of Personnel Management) Consultancy Service
35 Camp Road
London SW19 4UX
081–946 9100

The Institute of Personnel Management keeps a list of personnel consultants who give career counselling to individuals. NB: This can be expensive.

Job Centres
Look in the phone book, or contact:

Employment Service Head Office
St Vincent's House
30 Orange Street
London WC2H 7HT
071–839 5600

Your local Job Centre will give you details of organisations which can help you. They usually carry a stock of useful leaflets about your rights and payments.

The Labour Relations Agency
Windsor House
9–15 Bedford Street
Belfast BT2 7NU
0232 321442

In Northern Ireland – for advice for employers and employees on any employment problem; they have an advice line.

Law Centres
Look in the phone book or contact the head office of the Law Centres Federation:
Duchess House
18/19 Warren Street
London W1P 5DB

They help on all aspects of redundancy.

The Law Society of England and Wales
113 Chancery Lane
London WC2A 1PL
071–241 1222

The Law Society of Northern Ireland
Law Society House
98 Victoria Street
Belfast BT1 3JZ
0232 231614

The Law Society of Scotland
26 Drumsheugh Gardens
Edinburgh EH3 7YR
031–226 7411

Local Enterprise Councils
Equivalent in Scotland of Training and Enterprise Councils (see below).

Local Enterprise Development Unit (LEDU)
LEDU House
Upper Galwally
Belfast BT8 4TB
0232 491031

Low Pay Unit
29 Amwell Street
London EC1R 1UN
071–713 7616

They give direct advice to people who have been made redundant.
They also produce fact sheets.

Money Advice Units
Look in the phone book for details.

National Association of Volunteer Bureaux
St Peter's College
College Road
Saltley
Birmingham B8 3NE
021–327 0265

For information on the whereabouts of your local Volunteer Bureau
and the help they can give, ask your local CAB.

New Ways to Work
309 Upper Street
London N1 2TY
071–226 4026

Produces leaflets on job-sharing and can put you in touch with job-sharing groups around the country.

Northern Ireland Small Business Unit
Enterprise House
University of Ulster
Gordonstown
Newtownabbey BT37 0QB

OPAS (The Occupational Pensions Advisory Service)
11 Belgrave Road
London SW1V 1RB
071–233 8080

Provides advice through a network of advisers around the country, on problems with occupational pensions.

Open College
St Paul's
781 Wilmslow Road
Didsbury
Manchester M20 8RW
061-434 0007
or
Second Floor
300 Newtownards Road
Belfast BT4 1HE
0232 453990

Runs courses leading to vocational qualifications.

Open University
Central Enquiry Service
PO Box 71
Milton Keynes MK7 6YZ
0908 274066
Scotland 031-225 2889

Runs courses leading to vocational qualifications.

Redundancy Payments Service
Free advice line: 0800 848489

Relate
Look in the phone book or contact their head office:
Herbert Gray College
Little Church Street
Rugby
Warwickshire CV21 3AP
0788 573241

This is the new name of the Marriage Guidance Council. They deal with family relationships, not just marriage problems.

Social Security
Freephone: 0800 666555

This is a free phone line for information about benefits and national insurance.

Tax Offices
Look under Inland Revenue in the phone book or ask your CAB.

Your local tax office can give you advice about the tax position regarding your redundancy payment.

Training and Employment Agency
Gloucester House
57–63 Chichester Street
Belfast BT1 2RA
0232 235211

Training and Enterprise Councils (TECs); Local Enterprise Councils (LECs) in Scotland; Training and Employment Agency in Northern Ireland
Look in the phone book or ask at the CAB, Job Centre, library or Careers Service. For information about setting up in business or going self-employed phone 0800 222999 and ask for Freephone Enterprise.

Section B

British Executive Services Overseas (Beso)
164 Vauxhall Bridge Road
London SW1V 2RB
071-630 0644

Beso is backed by the Ministry for Overseas Development, the CBI
and the IOD. It could be worth talking to if you are interested in an
executive appointment in Eastern Europe or in the Third World.

Chambers of Commerce
Look in the phone book or ask at the CAB or library. Could be a
useful source of information – particularly about local job clubs,
etc.

Exhibition Bulletin
Published monthly by:
The London Bureau
226–272 Kirkdale
Sydenham
London SE26 4RZ
081-778 2288

Details of relevant exhibitions.

Federation of Small Businesses
0235 720911
Provides a useful fact sheet on establishing a small business.

Graduate Advisory Service
Every (as far as I know) university and college of higher education has
its own Graduate Advisory Service – and they are all linked together
by the Association of Graduate Advisory Services. Approach the
service through your own university or college.

Institute of Directors
116 Pall Mall
London SW1Y 5ED
071-839 1233

This has an excellent range of services for members. I am not suggesting
that your recent redundancy makes this the ideal time to join, but if

you have a contact who is a member you may be able to glean some useful information. IOD is also influential in many areas of interest to top executives, including non-executive directorships and temporary management assignments.

Institute of Personnel Management
Details at Section A. IPM is the professional institute most closely concerned with the personnel aspects of redundancy, and produces many useful books, pamphlets and journal articles on this and related topics.

MBA *Career Guide*
49 Murray Mews
Camden
London NW1 9RH

Produces a comprehensive guide to MBA courses.

Ownbase
081-363 0808

A national network for home-based workers which issues a newsletter and produces a trading directory.

Appendix 2

Advertisements in the National Press

Notes: a. As explained in chapter 10, you will find advertisements in the national press, in the local press and in specialist journals/magazines/newsletters/newspapers, etc. This appendix is concerned solely with the national press.

b. Papers are listed alphabetically. Depending on your specialisation and style you will, from the information here, be able to draw up your personal list of what papers to scan on what days.

c. Things change – so check that the information you extract from the following pages is still correct.

d. Certain papers use the system of double insertion (e.g. *Daily Telegraph/Sunday Telegraph*, *The Times/Sunday Times*, *Independent/Independent on Sunday*). Indeed, some advertisements appear three times (e.g. *Daily Telegraph* on Thursday, *Daily Telegraph* on Saturday, and *Sunday Telegraph*). However, you can rarely be certain that any specific advertisement will be repeated, so it is best to see all the appropriate papers.

e. The word 'general' is used when non-specific appointments are included. 'All' means all classifications.

Daily Express	Tuesday	General
		Building/Construction
		Catering/Hotels
		Public Sector
		Secretarial
		Financial Sales
		Training & Tuition
		Retail
	Wednesday	Creative & Media
		Sales & Marketing
	Thursday	Engineering/Technology
		Public Sector
		Retail
Daily Mail	Thursday	All
Daily Star	Thursday	Building/Construction
		Engineering
		Sales
		Training & Tuition
Daily Telegraph	Tuesday	All
	Thursday	General
	(main day)	Executive
		Educational
	Saturday	Executive Appointments
European	Weekly	All
Financial Times	Wednesday	Banking
		Finance
		General
	Thursday	Accountancy
	Friday	International edition – all appointments which have appeared on Wednesday and Thursday appear as one section in the edition on Friday.
Guardian	Monday	Creative & Media
		Marketing
		Secretarial
	Tuesday	Education
		International

	Wednesday	Public Sector
	Thursday	Science & Technology
		Computing
		Finance
		General
	Friday	Public Sector
		Housing
		Environment
Herald	Monday	All
	Wednesday	Education
		All
	Friday	All
	(Highest volume day)	
		Sales & Marketing
Independent	Monday	Computing
		Engineering
		Science & Technology
	Tuesday	Accountancy
		Finance
		Secretarial &
		European
	Wednesday	Media & Creative
		Sales & Marketing
	Thursday	Graduate
		Public Sector
		Education
		General
	Friday	Legal
Independent on Sunday	Sunday	All
Observer	Sunday	All
Scotsman	Monday	General
	Tuesday	General
	Wednesday	Education
	(best day)	General
	Thursday	General
		Public Sector

	Friday (main day)	General Sales & Marketing
Sunday Telegraph	Sunday	Direct repeat of Thursday's appointments supplement
Sunday Times	Sunday	All
The Times	Monday	Education Secretarial
	Tuesday	Legal Public Sector Creative & Media
	Wednesday	Secretarial
	Thursday	General Accountancy Finance Secretarial
	Friday	International Education Technical Commercial Academic
Today	Tuesday	All
	Thursday	All

*   *   *

Classification	Publication	Day
Academic	*The Times*	Friday
Accountancy (see also Finance)	*Financial Times* *Financial Times** *Independent* *The Times*	Thursday Friday Tuesday Thursday
Banking	*Financial Times* *Financial Times**	Wednesday Friday

---

* International edition – all appointments which have appeared on Wednesday and Thursday appear as one section in the international edition on Friday.

Building/Construction	*Daily Express*	Tuesday
	Daily Star	Thursday
Catering/Hotels	*Daily Express*	Tuesday
Commercial	*The Times*	Friday
Computing	*Guardian*	Thursday
	Independent	Monday
Creative & Media	*Daily Express*	Wednesday
	Guardian	Monday
	Independent	Wednesday
	The Times	Tuesday
Education	*Daily Telegraph*	Thursday
	Guardian	Tuesday
	Herald	Wednesday
	Independent	Thursday
	Scotsman	Wednesday
	The Times	Monday
	The Times	Friday
Engineering/Technology	*Daily Express*	Thursday
(see also Science & Technology)	*Daily Star*	Thursday
	Independent	Monday
Environment	*Guardian*	Friday
Executive	*Daily Telegraph*	Thursday
	Daily Telegraph	Saturday
Finance (see also Accountancy)	*Financial Times*	Wednesday
	Financial Times*	Friday
	Guardian	Thursday
	Independent	Tuesday
	The Times	Thursday
Financial Sales	*Daily Express*	Tuesday
Graduate	*Independent*	Thursday

---

* International edition – all appointments which have appeared on Wednesday and Thursday appear as one section in the international edition on Friday.

Housing	*Guardian*	Friday
International	*Guardian*	Tuesday
	The Times	Friday
Legal	*Independent*	Friday
	The Times	Tuesday
Public Sector	*Daily Express*	Tuesday
	Daily Express	Thursday
	Guardian	Wednesday
	Guardian	Friday
	Independent	Thursday
	Scotsman	Thursday
	The Times	Tuesday
Retail	*Daily Express*	Tuesday
	Daily Express	Thursday
Sales & Marketing	*Daily Express*	Wednesday
	Daily Star	Thursday
	Guardian	Monday
	Herald	Friday
	Independent	Wednesday
	Scotsman	Friday
Science & Technology (see also Engineering/ Technology)	*Guardian*	Thursday
	Independent	Monday
Secretarial	*Daily Express*	Tuesday
	Guardian	Monday
	Independent	Tuesday
	The Times	Monday
	The Times	Wednesday
	The Times	Thursday
Technical	*The Times*	Friday
Training & Tuition	*Daily Express*	Tuesday
	Daily Star	Thursday

All		
	Daily Mail	Thursday
	Daily Telegraph	Tuesday
	European	Weekly
	Herald	Monday
	Herald	Wednesday
	Herald	Friday
	Independent on Sunday	Sunday
	Observer	Sunday
	Sunday Times	Sunday
	Today	Tuesday
	Today	Thursday
General		
	Daily Express	Tuesday
	Daily Telegraph	Thursday
	Financial Times	Wednesday
	Financial Times *	Friday
	Guardian	Thursday
	Independent	Thursday
	Scotsman	Monday
	Scotsman	Tuesday
	Scotsman	Wednesday
	Scotsman	Thursday
	Scotsman	Friday
	Sunday Telegraph †	Sunday
	The Times	Thursday

All   = All sectors covered
General = Non-specific appointments covered

---

* International edition – all appointments which have appeared on Wednesday and Thursday appear as one section in the international edition on Friday.
† Direct repeat of Thursday's appointments supplement.

Appendix 3

The World's Worst Letter?

John Smith's letter is repeated for your convenience.
To make the exercise more comprehensible I have categorised my comments as follows:

    A   Layout
    B   Accuracy
    C   Social solecisms
    D   Grammar
    E   Spelling
    F   Punctuation
    G   Eye for detail
    H   Understanding the recruitment process
    I   Helping the advertiser
    J   Image
    K   Style
    L   Shape

The numbers given to my comments refer to the line numbers in the left-hand margin of the example letter.

1 My ref: JS/ADVT/5072/92/37B   Mr John Smith
2   99 Waterfront Terrace
3   Casterwilge
4   Somerset
5
6 David McKintosh
7 96 Bonny Bray Square
8 Ochaythenoo
9 by Edinborough
10 EH99 1AZ
11
12 Dear Dave
13
14 I would like to apply for the advertised job
15 in your company.
16
17 I believe that your main criteria is good
18 line manager experience which I certainly have!
19
20 I have not got a CV but I can say that I meet
21 your requirement completely, however I could
22 generate a CV for your perusal if you need me.
23
24 I am looking for a job that will increase my
25 salary and other benefits.
26
27 I need a high quality "executive" car this is very
28 important to me for customer liason which I
29 I consider is in my companies interest.
30
31 I do not consider that location is a problem.
32
33 I left my last job following a "policy disagreement"

34 at my directors insistense
35
36 I note that you require a degree or similar qualification
37 but I dont agree, I have met a lot of very stupid
38 people with degrees and I think you have got
39 the job description wrong and I am sure that I
40 can convince you that it is wrong which as so often
41 happens in recruitmnt by people who dont understand
42 the industry which is why I have had 15 interviews
43 but no final interviews but there is so much bais
44 against people without degrees dont you agree
45
46 I do not want to currently tell you my salary
47 as I was "grosly underpaid" for political reasons
48 and I cannot am not able to because I have been
49 in a grate many jobs give you my salary
50 history because it was a long time ago but we can disscus
51 this criteria when we meet up.
52
53 I look forward to your reply in the very near
54 future so that I can meet with you?
55
56 Yours Faithfully
57
58 ~~~~~~~~~~~~~~
59
60 (JOHN SMITH (MR)
61
62
63 P.S I am soon going on a holiday for
64 3 weeks
65
66

A   Layout

1   These writer's references are pretentious rubbish and should be omitted.

1   Do not put your name in the address block.

—   Own telephone number?

—   Own post code?

—   Date?

6   Mr or Esq

56   If addressed by name, the ending should be 'Yours sincerely'. If 'Dear Sir', then 'Yours faithfully'; not 'Faithfully'.

58   An effort at a legible signature, please.

B   Accuracy

—   Silly inaccuracies are very common and not always from expected sources. I recently had a speculative letter from an MBA at a very long established university with three spelling mistakes on the envelope.

6   Spelling the recipient's name incorrectly is a major crime.

—   'Mackintosh Enterprises' omitted.

7   Two mistakes – pathetic.

8   And one more.

9   At least he ought to be able to spell Scotland's capital correctly.

10   With any luck it won't reach me.

C   Social Solecisms

1   Even if it were acceptable to put one's name here, it is never acceptable to refer to oneself as 'Mr'.

12   Bloody cheek. It is amazing how many people start their letters 'Dear David' rather than 'Dear Mr Mackintosh'. However, there is a problem with women – 'Miss', 'Mrs' or 'Ms'? I recommend a phone call to find out – but, if in doubt, use 'Miss' which is less likely to offend than 'Mrs' if one's got it wrong. At all costs avoid the appalling 'Ms'.

12   Abysmal. How dare Smith address me as 'Dave'?

60   Dotting a capital I is a certain indicator of an illiterate nincompoop.

60   See earlier comments about 'Mr'. On the other hand, it is helpful if women put 'Mrs' or 'Miss'. This may sound sexist, but it does help the recipient to address you correctly in future. Remember that your job is to make the recruiter's life as easy as possible.

D   Grammar

17   'Criteria' is plural; the singular is 'criterion'.

17   This is all pretty revolting stuff, but would be improved by 'line management experience', although a purist would rightly hate that also.

27   Appalling sentence.

36   This paragraph and grammar have nothing in common; detailed comment would be superfluous.

46   A split infinitive is not the end of the world, but should be avoided.

48   When we split 'em, we split 'em.

51   'Criteria' in the singular again.

E   Spelling

–   You should have no difficulty with these: 21, 25, 28, 34, 43, 47, 47, 49, 50.

F   Punctuation

18   Irrelevant use of an exclamation mark irritates most readers.

21   A lousy sentence needing something more than a comma and reshaping to avoid a futile 'however'.

25   The apostrophe appears to be dead. It is, of course, unnecessary here.

27   Superfluous inverted commas are now sweeping the nation like

33   the Black Death. They are the written equivalent of 'Y'know'

47   and 'I mean', and should be avoided.

–   Missing apostrophes aplenty: 34, 37, 41, 44.

G   Eye for Detail

60   This may seem trivial, but executives seeking well-paid jobs should get their detail right – e.g. two brackets open, but only one closes.

H   Understanding the Recruitment Process

Comments to date have been general to all letter-writing. We now move towards the specifics of answering advertisements.

15   A common error and an annoying one (it certainly annoys me). The advertisement states quite clearly that I am acting as a consultant to the company, i.e. I am recruiting for International Casinos plc and not for Mackintosh Enterprises.

39   Smith doesn't understand the difference between the job description (which describes the job) and the employee specification/candidate profile (which describes the person we seek).

I   **Helping the Advertiser**
         The advertiser has to screen 100, 200, 300 ... replies. If you
         don't do what he/she asked you to do, you are not going to get
         past that initial stage.

−   Candidates were asked to quote the reference number given in
         the advertisement. Without it, any letter may move straight from
         the in-tray to the reject pile.

14   Particularly if you don't say what the job is or where the
         advertisement appeared.

−   However, the real problem is that I have no method of assessing
         Smith's skills and experience against the specification.

17   A stupid paragraph. I am the judge of how good Smith's
         experience is, not he.

18   Smith isn't being a bit of help to me. In order to screen his
         application I need facts. He really needs a CV before he starts
         replying to advertisements.

31   What a cretin. He lives in Somerset and the job is based in the
         Isle of Wight. What does he mean by this? Does he mean that he
         will travel daily? Will he relocate? Will he acquire a *pied à terre*
         on the Isle of Wight? At whose expense? I am not suggesting he
         should go into all this here, but he should say enough − briefly −
         to set my mind at rest.

46   The advertisement asked for salary history. By refusing to provide
         this information Smith has killed his chance. He should aim to
         respond to my needs, not to antagonise me.

63   As an item of information to help me in my task this is brilliant.
         Holiday dates?

−   Finally, in this section, should letters be hand-written or typed?
         In general, typescript is easier to read quickly than manuscript,
         and speed is my main problem in screening. Hand-written letters
         are acceptable only if the fist is elegant.

J   **Image**
         All the above errors will give Smith a poor image in my eyes as I
         screen his application, but there are more specific indicators.

24   Smith is immersed in his wants rather than in solving my client's
         problems.

27   The car freak is usually a status-conscious pain.

33   Clearly Smith was fired, in which case he should avoid drawing
         my attention to that fact in this letter.

36   What a whinger. This paragraph may appear to be completely
         over the top, but it is amazing how often candidates tell me that
         everyone else is in the wrong. Am I surprised that Smith has

never been back for a second interview? No, I am certainly
not.

46   More of the same.

–   In any event, all these comments are superfluous because lined
paper is a no-no for most executive appointments.

K   Style

–   This letter contains ten paragraphs. Each one starts with 'I'. It is
amazing how often this mistake is made – even by reasonably
civilised people.

–   A prevalent disease in this country is to treat the paragraph and
the sentence as synonymous.

–   This point does not arise in Smith's letter because he has failed to
answer the requirements specified in the advertisement. Phrasing
should, wherever possible, be proactive, e.g. 'I was responsible
for' is preferable to 'responsibilities included'.

14   Why would he 'like to apply'? Why doesn't he just apply?

22   Many books and outplacement firms' instructions include lists of
OK-words for inclusion in letters and CVs. Many of these words
are useful; some are revolting. Leader of the latter group is
'generate'. For example, in the old days one would 'draft' or
'write' a letter, not 'generate' it. Leave the word alone.

22   When I see the phrase 'for your perusal', I know that I am
dealing with a peasant. Eschew it.

36   I am always pleased to be told that I don't know my job.

51   Can't we just meet?

53   The phrase 'in the very near future' is extremely threatening and
a complete turn off. I'll reply when I'm good and ready, thanks.

54   Again, can't we just meet?

L   Shape

You never read a letter without looking at it first.

–   Read that again – it is a paramount consideration when thinking
about letter-writing. (The same applies to the writing of CVs.)
Smith's letter breaks three rules concerning the shape of a letter:

a. It is on more than one page.
b. It looks scruffy.
c. The shape is not inviting. I explained this in more detail in
chapter 11.

In short, Smith's letter is not easy on the eye and I would not read it.

Appendix 4

Fifty Questions To Cut your Teeth On

Preliminary Notes

a. The purpose of producing a list such as this is *not* to allow you to prepare *verbatim* answers. Nothing is more irritating for an experienced interviewer than to watch the candidate's eyes glaze over as the brain is put into gear to retrieve a prepared answer from the memory bank.

b. Questions will rarely be asked exactly in the way for which you have prepared. In many interviews – I would go so far as saying in good interviews – the concept of question and answer gives way to a discussion, which covers the ground without actually seeming like a cross-examination.

c. I want you to use these questions – and your answers to them – to aid your thoughts, so that you can practise giving shape and clarity to your answers or your share of the dialogue.

d. A decision you must make during the interview is how much to talk. If the interviewer is competent, then the type of question will lead you to the right pace, in which case don't rabbit on. If, however, the interviewer appears to run out of steam very quickly, you should start to give lengthier answers which open up further areas. However, remember that many more interviews are lost by those who talk too much than by those who don't talk enough.

e. Various advisers will tell you to answer a question with a question. For example, I read one document recently which suggested that the correct answer to the question, 'Have you got a degree?' is not, 'Yes, a second in history from Faringdon University' because the interviewer may be seeking skills in, say, engineering. The author suggested that what you should say is, 'Yes, what background are you looking for?' If you've read this book assiduously, you'll know that this is rubbish. Asking a question in response to a question is pushy and not our British way. And what is the point of trying to conceal the discipline of your degree? It merely diminishes your very valid achievement.

f.   The questions are deliberately in random sequence. Few interviews go according to the interviewer's plan; practically never according to the candidate's plan. You must learn – or relearn – to think on your feet.

g.   Practise with anyone who'll give you the time – your counsellor, your spouse, your children or anyone you can bully into giving you a few moments.

h.   There are no right answers, only *your* answers. I have, however, added some footnotes to aid your thoughts.

i.   Not all the questions apply to all jobs – e.g. private *versus* public sector, experienced executive *versus* milk-round graduate.

*   *   *

1.   *Why did you go into engineering/accountancy/sales/the Navy/ teaching/the Civil Service/medicine/ ...?*

2.   *What have you learnt about yourself as a result of being made redundant?*

3.   *On reflection, do you think you chose the right university?*

4.   *On reflection, would you like to have read a different subject?*

5.   *If you could re-run your life, what one decision would you make differently?*

6.   *Would you please take me through the job changes in your working life, explaining your movements from one job to another?*

(NB: It is amazing how often this simple question leads to a lengthy – and often boring – life history. What I am looking for is a simple run-through of the movement pattern, mainly to help my overtaxed brain understand the career structure of the candidate. I ask this question when the candidate has had a busy movement pattern. I am looking for reassurance that he or she hasn't been fired at regular intervals. I would remind you that I, the interviewer, WANT YOU TO DO WELL, so I am seeking reassurance – and, of course, the truth.)

7.   *Do you think that appraisal systems should be linked to salaries – and why?*

8.   *Tell me about the most difficult boss you have ever had to deal with*

and how you handled the situation. What have you learnt from the experience?

9. *Tell me about the most difficult subordinate you have had to deal with and how you handled the situation. What have you learnt from the experience?*

10. *When you recruit staff to work for you, how do you go about it?*

11. *Why do you think you are right for this job?*

    (NB: This gives you a good chance to display your knowledge of the company from your research, by weaving it into your reply to this question.)

12. *What interests you most about this job?*

    (NB: Another way of approaching the substance of the last question.)

13. *If you had a really important social/family engagement, and the job required you to fly to Singapore and miss it, what would you do?*

    (NB: Very important you should display balance here. For example, if the very important social engagement is giving your daughter away at her wedding – or even being the bride or groom at your own wedding – it would be unreasonable to expect you to change the plans at short notice. The purpose of asking a question like this – it could be phrased in a variety of ways – is to ensure that one is dealing with a balanced person who would put the job first except on those occasions when the conflicting engagement should rightly take priority.)

14. *What mistakes have you made – and what have you learnt from them?*

15. *What, in your opinion, is the difference between leadership and management?*

16. *What are your views on the Schwartz-Metterklume method of management?*

    (NB: An example of an unanswerable question – to the best of my knowledge Schwartz-Metterklume does not exist outside Saki. I shall be very happy if you tell me that you've never heard of it.)

17. *Would you rather work for a man or a woman – and why?*

18. *What was the most interesting job you have done? Why?*

19. *Do you read books on management? What have you learnt from them?*

20. *Why aren't you earning more at your age?*

21. *If I were to ask your last secretary what she thought of you, and if (though I am sure she wouldn't necessarily) she were to give me a totally frank and honest answer, what would she say about your interpersonal relationships and your management style?*

22. *Have you faced up to the fact that this job will require you and your family to relocate?*

    (NB: This is something I have been hammering away at throughout the book. You resolved the relocation parameters early on, and you must not fumble this answer now.)

23. *Why are you prepared to work for less money than you were getting earlier?*

24. *Why do you think you are worth so much more money, in salary terms, than you were getting before?*

25. *How have you spent your vacations during your university years?*

26. *Would you like to have your present (or last) boss's job?*

27. *If I had to write your obituary today, what particular achievements in your working life should I mention?*

28. *Who is the best boss you ever worked for? What did you learn from him or her?*

29. *What do you perceive to be the differences between working for a private company and working for a public company?*

30. *Should credit control be the responsibility of sales or finance?*

31. *What went wrong in your last job?*

32. *What do you want to be doing in five years' time?*

33. *When could you start work?*

34. *How many other jobs are you in the running for at the moment?*

35. *Why have you undergone so little training and development during your career?*

36. *In view of the fact that you have spent all your working life in the public sector, why do you think your experience fits you for this job in the private sector?*

37. *In view of the fact that you have spent all your working life in the private sector, why do you think your experience fits you for this job in the public sector?*

38. *Let's discuss your years as projects director at LMN plc. What was the task you faced when you took over the appointment? What was your plan for achieving your objectives? What went well and what went less well? How might you have done even better with the benefit of hindsight?*

    (NB: A favourite of mine. Yes, I realise there are actually five questions here, but, when recruiting high-priced people, one expects them to be able to absorb all this, break down the topic to its appropriate parts, combine description and analysis and, putting all this together, say something really interesting. When interviewing candidates with lesser remunerative aspirations, I tend to take it much slower and by stages.)

39. *If I handed you a balance sheet, could you explain it to me?*

(NB: Two points here. First, it is a closed question, to which the simple answer is 'Yes' or 'No'. The textbooks say that interviewers should not ask closed questions. Personally I sometimes ask them if I have a particularly voluble candidate just to see if I can get a short answer to a closed question. Secondly, be wary. Don't say 'Yes' if you can't; you will be found out when a company report slides across the coffee table. It is much better to be honest: 'Not perfectly, but I think I could pull out the salient points', which leaves you in a nicely poised position.)

40. *What newspapers do you read?*

(NB: A more extreme example of a closed question. Keep it short and factual, e.g.: '*The Times* on weekdays and the *Sunday Telegraph*'. Don't embellish, unless you decide that you have a hopeless interviewer who asks a string of closed questions – in which case you will ease the situation if you explain your choice in an open-ended way.)

41. *The company is considering developing operations in America/ Australia/Japan, etc. – have you any general thoughts about the idea?*

42. *Have you any experience of doing business overseas? What cultural differences have you noticed in the business sense?*

43. *I see from your CV that you studied photosynthesis at university, some twenty years ago. What changes have taken place in that subject since then?*

44. *What is your greatest strength?*

45. *What is your greatest weakness?*

46. *I see that you have several leisure interests. How do you find time for them and work as well?*

47. *Have you any restrictions on travel?*

48. *Do you enjoy international business travel?*

(NB: Here is an example of a question that seeks an honest answer – well, they all do that, but this one discloses insincerity pretty quickly. Anyone who says, 'Yes, I love it – interminable queueing up at airports and security checks, staying in boring business hotels which are the same the whole world over, breakfast meetings and late nights, always rushing and never a chance to see where you are,' must be unhinged. An interviewer – who has probably been through the same sort of thing – is much more likely to warm to, 'Yes, funnily enough. In spite of the queueing up at airports and security checks, staying in boring business hotels which are the same the whole world over, breakfast meetings and

late nights, always rushing and never a chance to see where
you are, nonetheless it is, in a sense, exciting and, if it's a
part of the job, I do it willingly.' Sorry, I have broken my
rule — I am not here to give you answers — but I think you'll
take the point about combining honesty and a positive message.)

49. *What is the question you would least like me to ask?*
50. *How would you answer it?*

Index